At CGP, exams are in our DNA...

OK, so your Biology exams probably aren't the thing you're most looking forward to in life... but this CGP book will make them seem a lot less mysterious.

It's packed with exam-style questions for every topic in Edexcel's Grade 9-1 International GCSE Biology* course — plus two complete practice exam papers to make sure you're 100% ready for the real thing.

As if that wasn't helpful enough, we've also included step-by-step answers at the back of the book. The future's looking brighter already.

* It's great for the Biology parts of the Edexcel International GCSE Science Double Award too.

CGP — still the best! ☺

Our sole aim here at CGP is to produce the highest quality books — carefully written, immaculately presented and dangerously close to being funny.

Then we work our socks off to get them out to you — at the cheapest possible prices.

Contents

☑ Use the tick boxes to check off the topics you've completed.

Section 7 — Reproduction and Inheritance

Section 8 — Ecology and the Environment

Section 9 — Use of Biological Resources

Practice Papers

Published by CGP

Editors:
Sarah Armstrong, Katherine Faudemer and Emily Forsberg.

Contributor:
Paddy Gannon

With thanks to Susan Alexander and Glenn Rogers for the proofreading.

With thanks to Jan Greenway for the copyright research.

ISBN: 978 1 78294 675 5

DDT diagram on page 77 from Biological Science Combined Volume Hardback, 1990, Soper, Green, Stout, Taylor.
Cambridge University Press.

Data used to construct the graph on page 111 from R. Doll, R. Peto, J. Boreham, I Sutherland. Mortality in relation to smoking:
50 years' observations on male British doctors. BMJ 2004; 328: 1519. With permission from BMJ Publishing Group Ltd.

Clipart from Corel®
Illustrations by: Sandy Gardner Artist, email sandy@sandygardner.co.uk
Printed by Elanders Ltd, Newcastle upon Tyne

Based on the classic CGP style created by Richard Parsons.

How To Use This Book

- Hold the book <u>upright</u>, approximately <u>50 cm</u> from your face, ensuring that the text looks like <u>this</u>, not ꙅ!483. Alternatively, place the book on a <u>horizontal</u> surface (e.g. a table or desk) and sit adjacent to the book, at a distance which doesn't make the text too small to read.

- In case of emergency, press the two halves of the book together <u>firmly</u> in order to close.

- Before attempting to use this book, familiarise yourself with the following <u>safety information</u>:

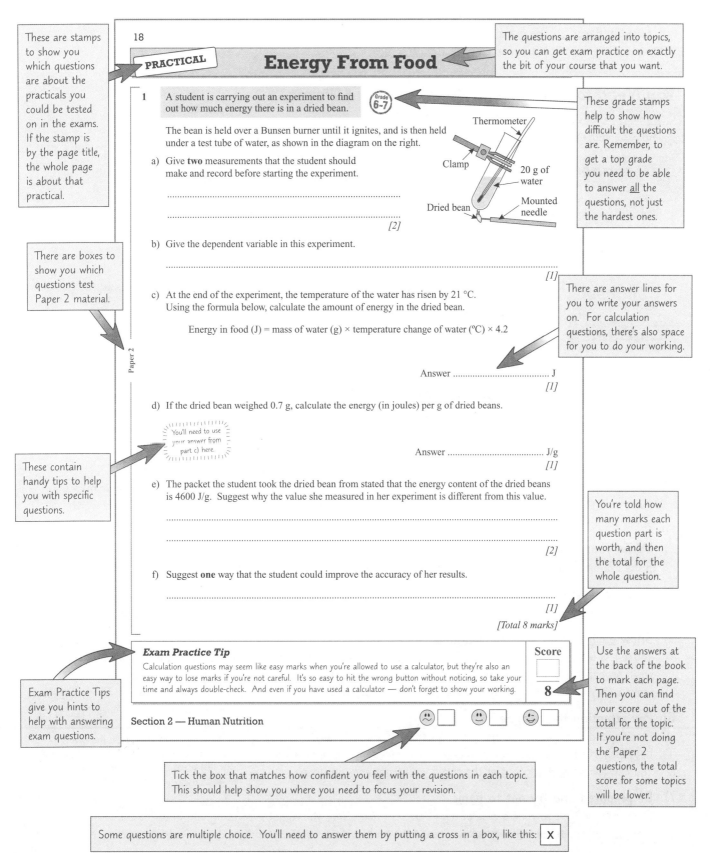

These are stamps to show you which questions are about the practicals you could be tested on in the exams. If the stamp is by the page title, the whole page is about that practical.

The questions are arranged into topics, so you can get exam practice on exactly the bit of your course that you want.

These grade stamps help to show how difficult the questions are. Remember, to get a top grade you need to be able to answer <u>all</u> the questions, not just the hardest ones.

There are boxes to show you which questions test Paper 2 material.

There are answer lines for you to write your answers on. For calculation questions, there's also space for you to do your working.

These contain handy tips to help you with specific questions.

You're told how many marks each question part is worth, and then the total for the whole question.

Exam Practice Tips give you hints to help with answering exam questions.

Use the answers at the back of the book to mark each page. Then you can find your score out of the total for the topic. If you're not doing the Paper 2 questions, the total score for some topics will be lower.

Tick the box that matches how confident you feel with the questions in each topic. This should help show you where you need to focus your revision.

18

PRACTICAL

Energy From Food

1 A student is carrying out an experiment to find out how much energy there is in a dried bean. *(Grade 6-7)*

The bean is held over a Bunsen burner until it ignites, and is then held under a test tube of water, as shown in the diagram on the right.

Thermometer
Clamp
20 g of water
Dried bean
Mounted needle

a) Give **two** measurements that the student should make and record before starting the experiment.

....
....
[2]

b) Give the dependent variable in this experiment.

....
[1]

c) At the end of the experiment, the temperature of the water has risen by 21 °C. Using the formula below, calculate the amount of energy in the dried bean.

Energy in food (J) = mass of water (g) × temperature change of water (°C) × 4.2

Answer .... J
[1]

d) If the dried bean weighed 0.7 g, calculate the energy (in joules) per g of dried beans.

You'll need to use your answer from part c) here.

Answer .... J/g
[1]

e) The packet the student took the dried bean from stated that the energy content of the dried beans is 4600 J/g. Suggest why the value she measured in her experiment is different from this value.

....
....
[2]

f) Suggest **one** way that the student could improve the accuracy of her results.

....
[1]
[Total 8 marks]

Exam Practice Tip

Calculation questions may seem like easy marks when you're allowed to use a calculator, but they're also an easy way to lose marks if you're not careful. It's so easy to hit the wrong button without noticing, so take your time and always double-check. And even if you have used a calculator — don't forget to show your working.

Score

8

Section 2 — Human Nutrition

Paper 2

Some questions are multiple choice. You'll need to answer them by putting a cross in a box, like this: **X**

Exam Tips

Before you get cracking on some exam practice, here's some handy information and some tips to help you in the exams.

Edexcel International GCSE Exam Stuff

1) For the Edexcel International GCSE in Biology, you'll sit two exam papers at the end of your course.

2) Some material in the specification will only be tested in Paper 2. The questions that cover Paper 2 material in this book are marked with a Paper 2 box.

Paper	Time	No. of marks
1	2 hours	110
2	1 hr 15 mins	70

You Need to Understand the Command Words

Command words are the words in a question that tell you what to do.
If you don't know what they mean, you might not be able to answer the questions properly.

Describe — This means you need to recall facts or write about what something is like.

Explain — You have to give reasons for something or say why or how something happens.

State — This means the same thing as 'Name...' or 'Give...'.
You usually just have to give a short definition or an example of something.

Suggest — You need to use your knowledge to work out the answer. It'll often be something you haven't been taught, but you should be able to use what you know to figure it out.

Calculate — This means you'll have to use numbers from the question to work something out.
You'll probably have to get your calculator out.

Seven Golden Rules for your Exam

1) Always, always, always make sure you read the question properly.
For example, if the question asks you to give your answer in mm, don't give it in cm.

2) **Look at the number of marks a question is worth.**
The number of marks gives you a pretty good clue of how much to write. So if a question is worth four marks, make sure you write four decent points. And there's no point writing an essay for a question that's only worth one mark — it's just a waste of your time.

3) **Write your answers as clearly as you can.**
If the examiner can't read your answer you won't get any marks, even if it's right.

4) **Use specialist vocabulary.**
You know the words I mean — the sciencey ones, like genotype and phenotype. Examiners love them.

5) **Show each step in your calculations.**
You're less likely to make a mistake if you write things out in steps. And even if your final answer's wrong, you'll probably pick up some marks if the examiner can see that your method is right. You also need to make sure you're working in the right units — check before you put any numbers in your calculator.

6) **Pay attention to the time.**
Don't spend ages staring at the question paper. If you're totally, hopelessly stuck on a question, just leave it and move on to the next one. You can always go back to it at the end if you've got enough time.

> Obeying these Golden Rules will help you get as many marks as you can in the exams — but they're no use if you haven't learnt the stuff in the first place. So make sure you revise well and do as many practice questions as you can.

7) **Be prepared and try not to panic.**
Exam day can give anyone a case of the jitters. So make sure you've got everything you need for the exam (pen, spare pen, pencil, ruler, calculator) ready the night before. Eat a good breakfast. And try to relax...

Characteristics of Living Organisms

1 Read the information below and answer the questions that follow.

The picture on the right shows an adult starfish. Starfish are found in oceans around the world. On the undersides of their arms they have small structures called 'tube feet', which are very sensitive to chemicals in the water, helping them to detect food. When they detect food, they move their arms to travel in the right direction. Each of their arms contains two gonads, which release eggs or sperm into the water.

a) Suggest and explain **three** pieces of evidence from the passage that show starfish are living organisms.

....

....

....

[3]

b) Suggest why starfish need to eat other organisms.

....

[1]

c) Name the process by which starfish release energy from the food they eat.

....

[1]

d) Starfish carry out the process of excretion. Describe what this means.

....

[1]

e) Suggest how a very young starfish may differ from the adult starfish shown above.

....

[1]

f) The fluid inside the body of a starfish has a different concentration of ions to the seawater around it. The starfish has special 'pumps' to keep the concentration of certain ions in its internal fluid at the right level. Explain how this is further evidence that a starfish is a living organism.

....

[1]

[Total 8 marks]

Exam Practice Tip

In the exams (usually in Paper 2) you could be given some information to read and then asked questions about it. Make sure you read both the passage and the questions very carefully. It's easy to lose marks by answering the question you think you've read rather than the one you've actually been asked.

Score

☐

8

 ☐   ☐   ☐

Levels of Organisation

1 All living organisms are made up of cells, which contain organelles. **Grade 4-6**

a) The cell nucleus is an organelle. Describe the structure of a cell nucleus.

....

....

[2]

b) Describe the function of:

i) chloroplasts

....

[1]

ii) the vacuole

....

[1]

c) Organelles and cells are the two smallest levels of organisation in multicellular organisms. List the next three levels in order of increasing size.

....

[2]

[Total 6 marks]

2 Plant and animal cells have similarities and differences. **Grade 4-6**

a) A plant cell is shown below.

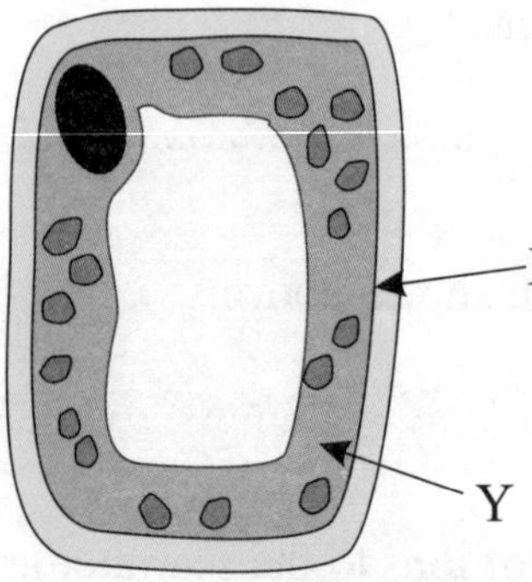

i) Name the parts of the cell labelled **X** and **Y**.

X ....

Y ....

[2]

ii) Add an arrow to the diagram to show where cellulose would be found within the cell.

[1]

b) Give **two** similarities and **two** differences between the structure of an animal cell and the structure of a plant cell.

Similarities: ....

....

Differences: ....

....

[4]

[Total 7 marks]

Score: [   ]

13

Section 1 — The Nature and Variety of Organisms

Specialised Cells and Stem Cells

1   As an organism develops, some of its cells develop different structures and change into different types of cells. This allows the cells to carry out specific functions. **Grade 4-6**

Which of the following processes describes this type of cell development?

☐ **A** mitosis   ☐ **B** adaptation   ☐ **C** differentiation   ☐ **D** specialisation

[Total 1 mark]

2   Treatments using embryonic stem cells may be able to cure many diseases. However, the use of embryonic stem cells in research and medicine is a controversial subject. Many governments around the world strictly regulate how they are used by scientists. **Grade 6-7**

a) It is hoped that stem cell treatment could be used in the future to treat patients with spinal injuries. Explain why embryonic stem cells have the potential to be used in the treatment of a patient paralysed by damage to cells in their spinal cord.

....

....

[2]

b) Lots of research is needed to overcome the challenges presented by using embryonic stem cells in medicine. Suggest a potential medical issue with the treatment suggested in part a).

....

....

[2]

c) Give **one** reason why some people are against using embryonic stem cells.

....

....

[1]

d) Stem cells can also be found in adult bone marrow.
Explain how these stem cells are different to embryonic stem cells.

....

....

[1]

[Total 6 marks]

Exam Practice Tip
You need to be familiar with the arguments for and against stem cell research. Stem cells have the potential to become one of many types of cell, so they could potentially be used to treat many diseases, such as diabetes and Parkinson's. But the use of embryonic stem cells raises real ethical issues.

Score

☐

7

 ☐   ☐   ☐

Paper 2

Plants, Animals and Fungi

1 A bean plant produces carbohydrate during photosynthesis. **(Grade 3-4)**

Which of the following organelles allows the cells of a bean plant to photosynthesise?

☐ **A** ribosome ☐ **B** chloroplast ☐ **C** cytoplasm ☐ **D** mitochondrion

[Total 1 mark]

2 *Mucor* and yeast are both fungi. **(Grade 6-7)**

a) Describe the structure of the mycelium of *Mucor*.

....

....

[2]

b) Which row of the table correctly shows two features of yeast?

		Feature 1	Feature 2
☐	**A**	Can store carbohydrate	Is multi-celled
☐	**B**	Is single-celled	Has cell walls containing chitin
☐	**C**	Can photosynthesise	Is single-celled
☐	**D**	Has cell walls containing chitin	Can photosynthesise

[1]

[Total 3 marks]

3 The growth of wheat plants can be slowed down by both fungi and insect pests. **(Grade 6-7)**

The table on the right shows information about the cells from both a fungus and an insect found on a wheat plant.

Feature	Organism A	Organism B
Chloroplasts present	No	No
Cell wall present	No	Yes
Glycogen store	Yes	Yes

a) Use information from the table to explain which organism (**A** or **B**) is an insect.

....

[1]

b) The fungus secretes enzymes onto the wheat, then absorbs the nutrients. State the name of this process.

....

[1]

c) Which organism (fungus or insect) can sense when it's on a source of food? Give a reason for your answer.

....

[1]

[Total 3 marks]

Score: ☐

7

☹ ☐   😐 ☐   🙂 ☐

Protoctists, Bacteria and Viruses

1   *Plasmodium* is a protoctist.   (Grade 3-4)

a)   Which of the following diseases is caused by *Plasmodium*?

☐ **A** pneumonia   ☐ **B** influenza   ☐ **C** malaria   ☐ **D** HIV

[1]

b)   The structure of *Plasmodium* is more similar to an animal cell than a plant cell.
Name another protoctist which has a similar structure to an animal cell.

....

[1]

[Total 2 marks]

2   The diagrams on the right show the bacteria
Lactobacillus bulgaricus and *Pneumococcus*.   (Grade 4-6)

A   **B**

a)   i)   Which diagram (**A** or **B**) shows *Lactobacillus bulgaricus*? Explain your answer.

....

[1]

ii) Describe how *Lactobacillus bulgaricus* can be used by the food industry.

....

[1]

b)   *Pneumococcus* is a pathogen. Explain what is meant by the term pathogen.

....

[1]

c)   Give **three** structural features of a typical bacterial cell.

....

....

[3]

[Total 6 marks]

3   Viruses can infect every type of living organism.   (Grade 6-7)

a)   The leaves of a tobacco plant can become discoloured if it is infected by a particular virus.
Name a virus that affects tobacco plants in this way and explain its effect.

....

....

[2]

b)   Name **one** virus that may infect humans and state the disease that it can cause.

....

[2]

Score:

[Total 4 marks]   **12**

Section 1 — The Nature and Variety of Organisms

Enzymes

1 Which row in the following table best describes enzymes?

	are affected by pH	speed up reactions	get used up during reactions	all have the same shape
☐ **A**	✓	✓		
☐ **B**			✓	
☐ **C**	✓	✓		✓
☐ **D**		✓	✓	✓

[Total 1 mark]

2 The diagram shows an enzyme before and after it has been exposed to a high pH.

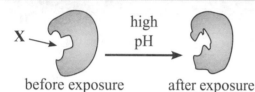

before exposure   after exposure

a) Name the part of the enzyme labelled **X**.

....

[1]

b) Explain how the high pH has affected the enzyme and how this will affect its activity.

....

....

....

....

[4]

[Total 5 marks]

3 Two different species of bacteria have slightly different versions of the same enzyme. Enzyme **A** is from a species of bacteria found in a hot thermal vent and enzyme **B** is from a species of bacteria found in soil. A scientist investigated the effect of temperature on the rate of reaction for both enzymes. The results are shown on the graph below.

Suggest which line represents enzyme **A**.
Give reasons for your answer.

....

....

....

....

....

....

....

Score: ☐

[Total 3 marks]

9

Investigating Enzyme Activity

1 The enzyme amylase is involved in the breakdown of starch into simple sugars.

A student investigated the effect of temperature on the activity of amylase in starch solution. Amylase and starch solution were added to test tubes X, Y and Z. The test tubes were placed in water baths of different temperatures, as shown in the table on the right.
Spotting tiles were prepared with a drop of iodine solution in each well. Iodine solution is a browny-orange colour but it turns blue-black in the presence of starch.

Test tube	Temp (°C)
X	32
Y	36
Z	48

Every 30 seconds, a drop of the solution from each of the test tubes was added to a separate well on a spotting tile. The resulting colour of the solution in the well was recorded in the table below.

Time (s)	30	60	90	120	150
Tube **X**	Blue-black	Blue-black	Blue-black	Browny-orange	Browny-orange
Tube **Y**	Blue-black	Browny-orange	Browny-orange	Browny-orange	Browny-orange
Tube **Z**	Blue-black	Blue-black	Blue-black	Blue-black	Blue-black

a) State the temperature at which the rate of reaction was greatest. Explain your answer.

....

....

....
[2]

b) Suggest an explanation for the results in tube **Z**.

....
[1]

c) Suggest **two** variables that should be controlled in this experiment.

....

....
[2]

d) The student repeated her experiment at 37 °C and got the same results as she got for her experiment at 36 °C. Suggest **one** way in which she could determine whether the rate of reaction is greatest at 36 °C or 37 °C.

....

....
[1]

e) The student carries out a similar experiment to investigate the effect of pH on amylase. Suggest how the student could vary the pH in a series of tubes containing the amylase and starch solution.

....

....
[1]   Score: ☐

[Total 7 marks]

7

☹ ☐   😐 ☐   😉 ☐

10

Diffusion

1 The diagram on the right shows a cell and the surrounding tissue fluid. Oxygen moves in and out of the cell by diffusion.

Grade 3-4

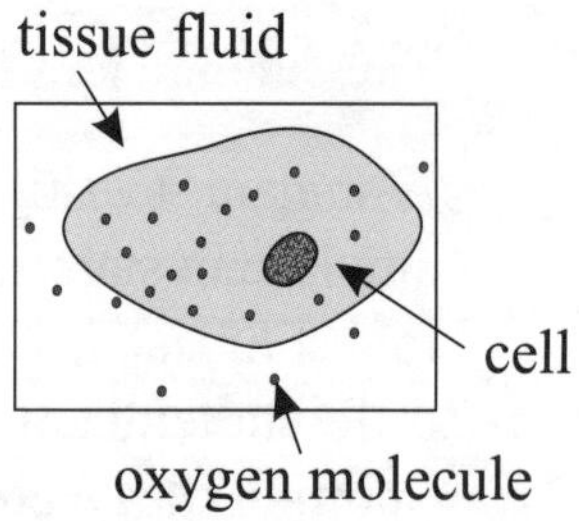

a) In which direction is the net movement of particles during diffusion?

- [ ] **A** From an area of low concentration to another area of low concentration.
- [ ] **B** From an area of low concentration to an area of high concentration.
- [ ] **C** From an area of high concentration to another area of high concentration.
- [ ] **D** From an area of high concentration to an area of low concentration.

[1]

b) Describe the effect that diffusion will have on the oxygen concentration inside this cell.

....
[1]

[Total 2 marks]

2 Diagram **A** below shows a cup of water which has just had a drop of dye added to it.

Grade 4-6

a) On diagram **B** below, draw the molecules of dye in the water after an hour.

A   **B**   *[1]*

b) Explain the movement of the dye particles in terms of differences in concentration.

....

....
[1]

[Total 2 marks]

3 A student was given three solutions labelled X, Y and Z. He placed equal amounts of each solution inside a bag designed to act like a cell membrane. He then put the bag inside a beaker of water. After 24 hours, the water outside the bag contained particles X and Y, but not Z.

Grade 4-6

What can you conclude about the relative sizes of the X, Y and Z particles? Explain your answer.

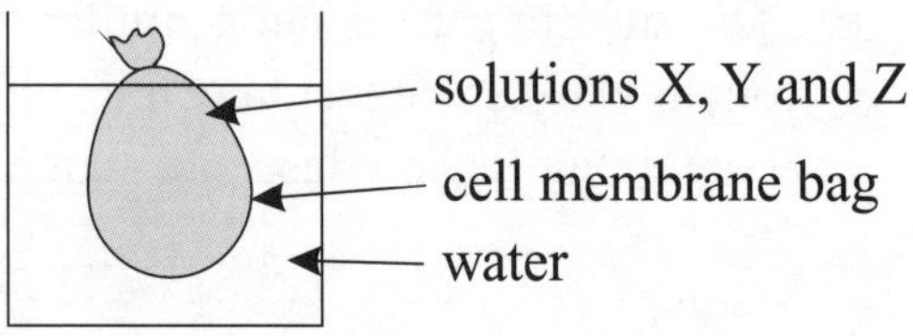

....

....
[Total 2 marks]

Section 1 — The Nature and Variety of Organisms

Score: [ ]

6

Osmosis

1 Osmosis is a form of diffusion. (Grade 4-6)

In which of the following scenarios is osmosis occurring?

☐ **A** Water is moving from the mouth down into the stomach.

☐ **B** Sugar is being taken up into the blood from the gut.

☐ **C** A plant is absorbing water from the soil.

☐ **D** Oxygen is entering the blood from the lungs.

[Total 1 mark]

2 The diagram below shows a tank divided in two by the structure labelled **X**. Osmosis will occur between the two sides of the tank. (Grade 4-6)

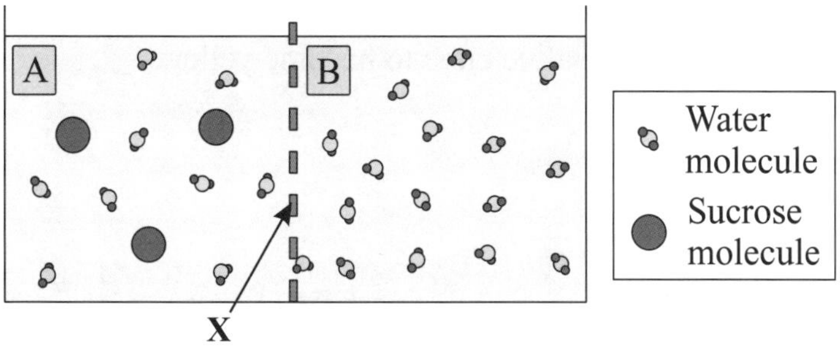

Water molecule

Sucrose molecule

X

a) Name the structure labelled **X** on the diagram.

....

....

[1]

b) Explain what will happen to the level of liquid on side **B**.

....

....

[2]

[Total 3 marks]

3 The diagram below shows some body cells bathed in tissue fluid. A blood vessel flows close to the cells, providing water. The cells shown have a low concentration of water inside them. (Grade 6-7)

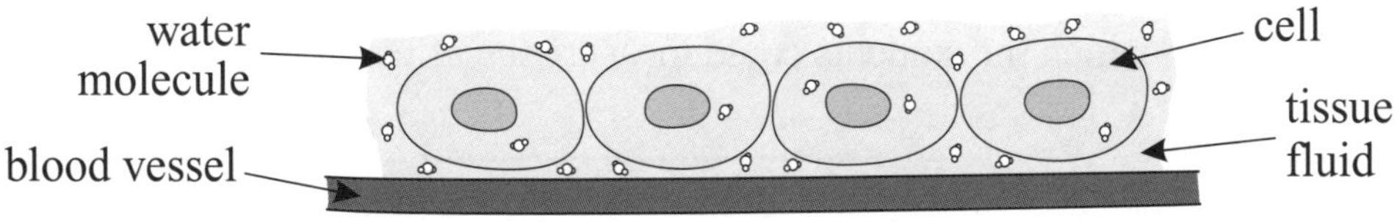

water molecule

blood vessel

cell

tissue fluid

a) Explain whether the net movement of water would be into or out of the body cells.

....

....

[2]

b) In the example above, suggest why osmosis appears to stop after a while.

....

....

[1]

Score: ☐

7

[Total 3 marks]

☹ ☐ 🙂 ☐ 😊 ☐

PRACTICAL — Diffusion and Osmosis Experiments

1 A student made up some gelatine with cresol red solution and ammonium hydroxide. Cresol red solution is a pH indicator that is red in alkaline solutions and yellow in acidic solutions. He cut the gelatine into cubes of different sizes, and placed the cubes in a beaker of dilute hydrochloric acid. He measured how long it took for the cubes to change from red to yellow as the acid moved into the gelatine and neutralised the ammonium hydroxide. His results are shown in the table.

Size (mm)	Time taken for cube to become yellow (s)			
	Trial 1	Trial 2	Trial 3	Trial 4
$5 \times 5 \times 5$	174	167	177	182
$7 \times 7 \times 7$	274	290	284	292
$10 \times 10 \times 10$	835	825	842	838

a) Name the process by which hydrochloric acid moves into the gelatine cubes in this experiment.

....

[1]

b) Calculate the average time for a $10 \times 10 \times 10$ mm gelatine cube to become yellow in this experiment. Show your working.

.... s

[2]

c) Explain the relationship between the size of the gelatine cube and the time taken for the cube to become yellow.

Bigger cubes have a smaller surface area : volume ratio.

....

....

[3]

[Total 6 marks]

2 Soaking an egg in vinegar dissolves its outer shell and leaves the egg surrounded by a partially permeable membrane. Some students use eggs which have been prepared in this way to investigate osmosis. They remove two eggs from the vinegar and place one of the eggs in a jar of water and the other in a jar of weak sugar solution.

Grade 7-9

a) Describe **one** way in which the students could measure the effect of osmosis.

....

....

[2]

b) Suggest what the results of this experiment would be.

....

....

[2]

c) Suggest a possible control for this experiment.

....

[1]

[Total 5 marks]

3 A student is investigating osmosis. She sets up an experiment as shown below, putting a different concentration of sucrose solution into each beaker. She put the same concentration of sucrose solution (0.2 M) into each length of Visking tubing.

Grade 7-9

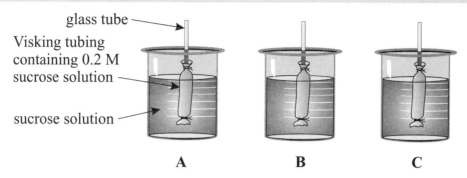

glass tube

Visking tubing containing 0.2 M sucrose solution

sucrose solution

A   B   C

The student records the level of the sucrose solution in each beaker at the start of the experiment and then again after 4 hours. Her results are shown in the table below.

Beaker	Change in level of sucrose solution in beaker (mm)
A	+ 3
B	0
C	− 2

a) Use information from the table to explain which beaker contained the following concentrations of sucrose solution:

Look carefully at the diagram — the concentration of sucrose solution inside the Visking tubing is 0.2 M.

i) 0.2 M ....

....

....

[2]

ii) 0.0 M ....

....

....

A sucrose solution of 0.0 M is just pure water.

[2]

b) Give **two** variables that need to be kept constant in this experiment.

1 ....

2 ....

[2]

c) Give **one** way in which the reliability of the experiment could be increased.

....

[1]

[Total 7 marks]

Exam Practice Tip

In your exams, you could easily be given an unfamiliar experiment to answer questions about. Don't panic. All you need to do is apply your existing scientific knowledge (e.g. about how osmosis works) and you'll be fine. Any extra information you need to answer the question should be given in the question itself. Phew.

Score

18

Section 1 — The Nature and Variety of Organisms

Active Transport

1   Two germinating barley seedlings were placed in solutions that contained a known concentration of potassium ions, as shown in the diagram below. Each seedling was grown at a different temperature. The uptake of potassium ions was measured.

Barley seedlings take up potassium ions by active transport.

a) Explain what is meant by the term **active transport**.

....

.... [2]

Seedling **A**   Seedling **B**

barley seedling

solution containing potassium ions

b) Use terms from the box to complete the table, showing which type of variable each factor is.

independent   dependent   control

Factor	Type of variable
Temperature	....
Concentration of potassium ion solution	....
Initial size of seedling	....
Rate of potassium ion uptake	....

[4]

c) The graph below shows the uptake of potassium ions by the barley seedlings.

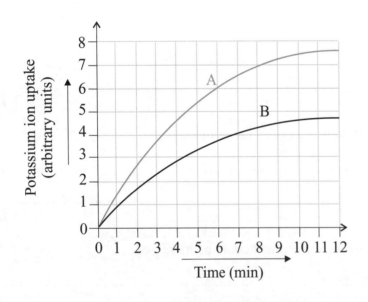

i) What is the potassium ion uptake for seedling **A** after 10 minutes?

.... arbitrary units [1]

ii) Suggest which seedling was grown at the higher temperature. Explain your answer.

....

....

....

.... [2]

d) Describe the effect that increasing the concentration of the potassium ion solution would have on the uptake of potassium ions via active transport.

.... [1]

[Total 10 marks]

Score: **10**

Biological Molecules

1 The elements below make up different biological molecules. *Grade 4-6*

    1. carbon
    2. hydrogen
    3. nitrogen
    4. oxygen

Which of these elements make up lipids?

  ☐ **A** 2, 3 and 4 only   ☐ **C** 1 and 4 only

  ☐ **B** 1, 2 and 4 only   ☐ **D** 1 and 2 only

[Total 1 mark]

2 Cell membranes contain structures called glycoproteins. As shown in the diagram below, glycoproteins are composed of both protein and carbohydrate. *Grade 4-6*

The cell uses enzymes to regularly break down and rebuild glycoproteins.

a) State the basic unit produced when the cell breaks down the carbohydrate portion of glycoproteins.

    ....

[1]

    ← carbohydrate

    ← protein

b) State the basic unit that the cell needs in order to rebuild the protein portion of glycoproteins.

    ....

[1]

[Total 2 marks]

3 Some bacterial species produce lipase (an enzyme that breaks down lipids). Two different species of bacteria were placed separately on an agar plate. The agar contained a lipid which made it cloudy. The plate was then left overnight. The results are shown in the diagram. *Grade 7-9*

  cloudy agar

  clear zone of agar

  bacterial species A

  bacterial species B

Use the diagram to suggest which species of bacteria contains lipase. Explain your answer.

....

....

....

[Total 2 marks]

Score: ☐

5

 ☐   ☐   ☐

Food Tests

1 A student was given test tubes containing the following glucose concentrations: 0 M, 0.02 M, 0.1 M, 1 M. The test tubes were not labelled and he was asked to perform tests to determine which test tube contained which glucose solution.

Grade 6-7

a) Describe the test he could carry out to try and distinguish between the glucose solutions.

....

....

....

....

....

[3]

b) The table shows the substance observed in the test tubes following his tests. Complete the table to show which glucose solution (0 M, 0.02 M, 0.1 M, 1 M) each test tube contained.

	Tube 1	Tube 2	Tube 3	Tube 4
substance observed	yellow precipitate	blue solution	red precipitate	green precipitate
glucose concentration (M)	....	....	....	....

[1]

[Total 4 marks]

2 A student is analysing the nutrient content of egg whites.

Grade 7-9

Fully describe an investigation that the student could carry out to find out if protein is present in a sample of cooked egg whites.

....

....

....

....

....

....

....

....

[Total 6 marks]

Exam Practice Tip

There's a lot to remember about the different food tests — the molecule being tested for, the reagent and method used, and the results. If food tests come up in the exam, think through what you're going to write before you start scribbling it all down — it's easy to get things a bit muddled in the heat of the moment.

Score

[ ]

10

Section 2 — Human Nutrition

A Balanced Diet

1   The body needs certain nutrients to help it to function properly.   (Grade 4-6)

a) Which of the following pairs of nutrients are used to provide energy for the body?

☐ **A** carbohydrates and dietary fibre   ☐ **C** lipids and iron

☐ **B** carbohydrates and lipids   ☐ **D** protein and dietary fibre

[1]

b) Mineral ions are essential nutrients for the body. Give **one** function of:

i) Iron ....

[1]

ii) Calcium ....

[1]

c) Give **one** example of a food that contains dietary fibre.

....

[1]

[Total 4 marks]

2   Different people have different energy requirements.   (Grade 6-7)

Calories are a measure of the amount of energy in food.

a) It is suggested that on average, non-pregnant women aged 19-49 need about 2000 calories per day, but most pregnant women in the same age group need 300 calories per day more. Explain why.

....

....

[1]

b) It is recommended that a 14-year-old girl with an average activity level should eat around 2000 calories per day. A woman over the age of 50 with an average activity level should eat around 1800 calories per day. Suggest **one** reason for why there is a difference.

....

....

[1]

c) Regardless of energy requirements, it is important that everyone has a balanced diet. Explain what is meant by the term **balanced diet**.

....

....

[2]

[Total 4 marks]

Score: ☐

8

 ☐   ☐   ☐

Section 2 — Human Nutrition

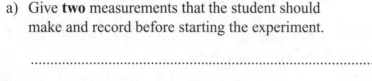

PRACTICAL — **Energy From Food**

1 A student is carrying out an experiment to find out how much energy there is in a dried bean.

Grade 6-7

The bean is held over a Bunsen burner until it ignites, and is then held under a test tube of water, as shown in the diagram on the right.

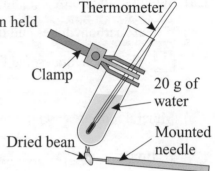
Thermometer
Clamp
20 g of water
Dried bean
Mounted needle

a) Give **two** measurements that the student should make and record before starting the experiment.

....

....
[2]

b) Give the dependent variable in this experiment.

....
[1]

c) At the end of the experiment, the temperature of the water has risen by 21 °C. Using the formula below, calculate the amount of energy in the dried bean.

Energy in food (J) = mass of water (g) × temperature change of water (°C) × 4.2

Answer .... J
[1]

d) If the dried bean weighed 0.7 g, calculate the energy (in joules) per g of dried beans.

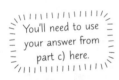
You'll need to use your answer from part c) here.

Answer .... J/g
[1]

e) The packet the student took the dried bean from stated that the energy content of the dried beans is 4600 J/g. Suggest why the value she measured in her experiment is different from this value.

....

....
[2]

f) Suggest **one** way that the student could improve the accuracy of her results.

....
[1]

[Total 8 marks]

Exam Practice Tip

Calculation questions may seem like easy marks when you're allowed to use a calculator, but they're also an easy way to lose marks if you're not careful. It's so easy to hit the wrong button without noticing, so take your time and always double-check. And even if you have used a calculator — don't forget to show your working.

Score

[ ]
———
8

Enzymes and Digestion

1   There are a number of digestive enzymes found in the human body.

Use the words from the box to complete the table, showing the correct enzyme or function in each space provided.

amylase   lipases   glycerol   maltase   amino acids

Enzyme	Function
proteases	convert proteins into ....
....	converts starch into maltose
....	converts maltose into glucose
....	convert lipids into fatty acids and ....

[Total 5 marks]

2   Gallstones are small, solid stones formed mainly of excess cholesterol. They can block the bile ducts (tubes) that connect the liver to the gall bladder and the gall bladder to the small intestine.

a) i) Name the digestive fluid stored in the gall bladder.

....

[1]

ii) Name the organs in the body where this digestive fluid is produced, and where it acts on food.

Produced ....   Acts ....

[2]

iii)This digestive fluid is alkaline. Explain why this is important.

....

....

[2]

b) Suggest why eating fatty foods might cause a problem for people suffering from gallstones.

....

....

....

....

[4]

[Total 9 marks]

Score:

14

The Alimentary Canal

1 The diagram shows the human alimentary canal, with different parts named or labelled with a letter (**A-F**).

(Grade 4-6)

a) Describe the function of the pancreas in digestion.

....

....

....

....

[2]

b) Complete the table by writing the letter of the label next to the correct function.

Function	Label letter
Pummels the food, and produces the protease enzyme pepsin.	....
Contains salivary glands, which produce amylase.	....
Where nutrients are absorbed from food.	....

[3]

c) Name the part of the alimentary canal where villi are found.

....

[1]

[Total 6 marks]

2 Irritable Bowel Syndrome (IBS) is a condition affecting the colon, where peristalsis occurs either too quickly or too slowly.

(Grade 7-9)

a) Describe the purpose of peristalsis in the alimentary canal.

....

....

[2]

b) When peristalsis happens too fast, it can lead to diarrhoea, where faeces are passed in liquid form. Suggest how rapid peristaltic action can cause diarrhoea in people with IBS.

....

....

....

[2]

[Total 4 marks]

Score:

10

Photosynthesis

1   The diagram shows a cross-section through a typical leaf. Some of the structures in the leaf are labelled **A** to **E**.

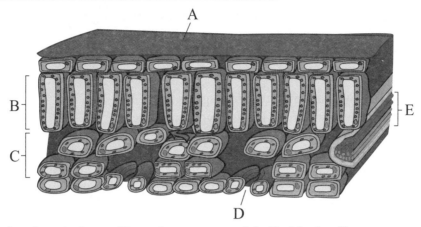

The table contains descriptions of how the structures labelled in the diagram make the leaf well-adapted for efficient photosynthesis.

Complete the table by matching the letters in the diagram to the correct description. The first one has been done for you.

Description of structure	Letter
contains air spaces to aid gas exchange	C
delivers water and nutrients to every part of the leaf	....
helps to reduce water loss by evaporation	....
where most of the chloroplasts in the leaf are located, to maximise the amount of light they receive	....
allows carbon dioxide to diffuse directly into the leaf	....

[Total 4 marks]

2   Photosynthetic organisms use photosynthesis to produce their own food.   Grade 6-7

a)   Explain how photosynthesis is involved in creating a store of chemical energy for the plant.

....

....

[2]

b)   i)   Write down the word equation for photosynthesis.

....

[2]

ii)   Write down the balanced symbol equation for photosynthesis.

....

[2]

Score: ☐

[Total 6 marks]

10

 ☐   ☐   ☐

Rate of Photosynthesis

1 A farmer in the UK doesn't put his cows out during the winter because the grass is not growing.

Grade 4-6

a) Suggest how the rate of photosynthesis and the growth rate of grass are related.

....

[1]

b) Suggest **two** reasons why the growth rate of grass in the UK is lower in winter than in summer. Explain your answer.

....

....

....

[3]

[Total 4 marks]

2 A student carried out an experiment to investigate the effect of different concentrations of carbon dioxide on the rate of photosynthesis of his Swiss cheese plant. The results are shown on the graph below.

Grade 6-7

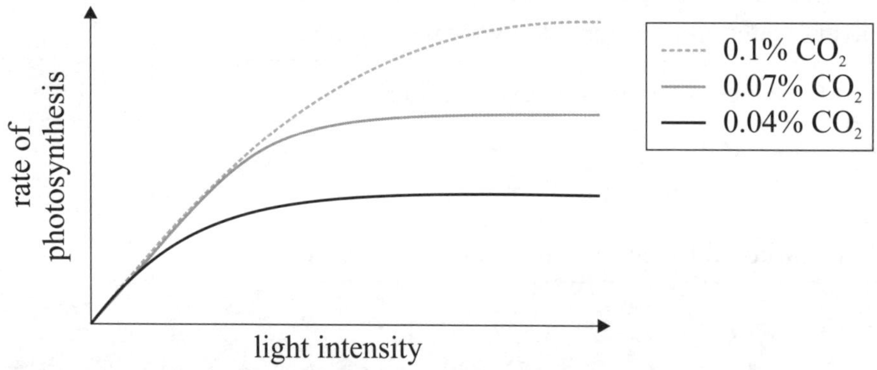

legend:
- - - - 0.1% CO_2
——— 0.07% CO_2
——— 0.04% CO_2

y-axis: rate of photosynthesis
x-axis: light intensity

a) Describe the effect that increasing the concentration of CO_2 has on the rate of photosynthesis as light intensity increases.

....

....

....

[2]

b) Explain why all the lines on the graph level off eventually.

....

....

[1]

[Total 3 marks]

3   Average daytime summer temperatures in different habitats around the world are shown in the table.

Habitat	Temperature (°C)
Forest	19
Arctic	0
Desert	32
Grassland	22
Rainforest	27

a) Plot a bar chart for this data on the grid below.

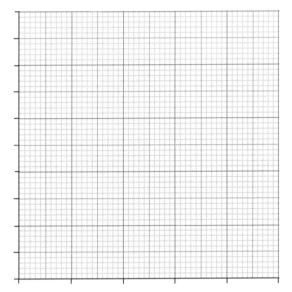

[4]

b) From the values for temperature, state the habitat in which you would expect fewest plants to grow. Explain your answer.

....

....

....

....

[4]

c) In dense rainforest, plants that grow close to the forest floor tend to have lower rates of photosynthesis than the very tall trees. Suggest why this might be.

....

....

[2]

[Total 10 marks]

Exam Practice Tip

Don't forget the basics when plotting graphs. Always label your axes (including any units), use a ruler for drawing straight lines, make sure the graph takes up at least half the grid you've been given to draw it on, and if your graph needs one, include a key. This can gain you a few marks before you've even touched the data.

Score

17

Photosynthesis Experiments

1 A student seals a plant in a bell jar containing a dish of soda lime. Soda lime absorbs carbon dioxide. The plant is left for 48 hours at room temperature. It begins to turn yellow and dies, despite getting lots of light, water and minerals.

Grade 4-6

a) Suggest what the results of this experiment tell you about photosynthesis.

....

[1]

b) Suggest why it is important that the plant is kept at room temperature and given plenty of light, water and minerals during the experiment.

....

....

[1]

[Total 2 marks]

2 A green leaf was boiled in water to soften it, and then boiled in ethanol. It was washed with water and some brown iodine solution was dropped onto it. The extra iodine solution was washed away.

Grade 6-7

a) The ethanol in the experiment turned green and the leaf went white. Suggest why this happened.

....

[1]

b) When the iodine was added to the leaf, it turned blue-black. Explain what this result shows.

....

[1]

The method above was repeated with the leaf shown below.

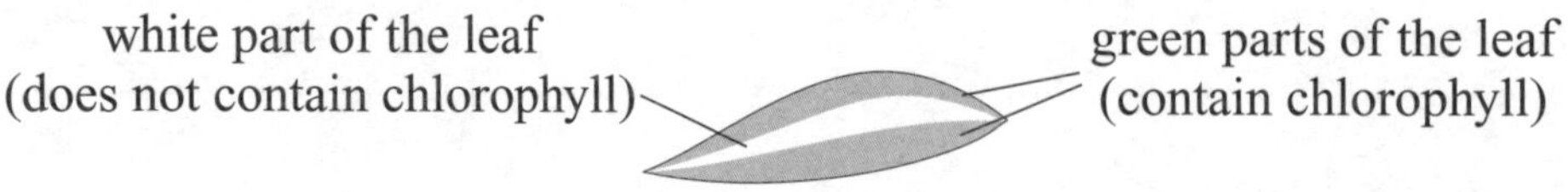

white part of the leaf
(does not contain chlorophyll)   green parts of the leaf
                                     (contain chlorophyll)

c) Explain the result you would expect to see when the leaf was tested with iodine solution.

....

....

....

....

....

[4]

[Total 6 marks]

3 A student investigated the volume of oxygen produced by pondweed at different intensities of light. Her results are shown in the table below.

Relative light intensity	1	2	3	4	5	6	7	8	9	10
Volume of oxygen evolved in 10 minutes (cm³)	8	12	18	25	31	13	42	48	56	61

a) Plot a graph of the student's results on the grid provided.

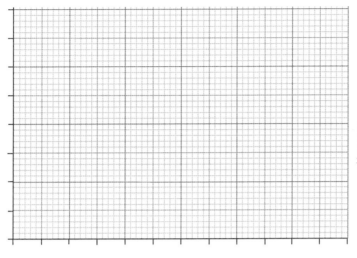

Remember: when you're plotting a graph of results like this, put the _dependent variable_ (the thing you measure) on the _vertical axis_.

[3]

b) i) One of the student's results is probably wrong.
   At which relative light intensity is the result likely to be wrong? ....

   [1]

   ii) Suggest **one** error that the student might have made when she collected this result.

   ....

   [1]

c) Describe what the student's results show about the relationship
   between light intensity and rate of photosynthesis.

   ....

   [1]

[Total 6 marks]

4 Describe an investigation to show that light is a requirement of photosynthesis.

....

....

....

....

....

....

[Total 6 marks]

Score: ☐

20

Section 3 — Plant Nutrition and Transport

26

Minerals for Healthy Growth

1 A gardener has noticed that his tomato crop is not growing well. He thinks this is due to a lack of nitrate ions in the soil.

Grade 4-6

Explain why a lack of nitrate ions could affect the growth of the tomato plants.

....

....

[Total 2 marks]

2 A scientist carried out an investigation into the magnesium requirements of plants. He planted 10 seedlings of the same variety in a growth medium containing a complete supply of minerals. He then planted a further 10 seedlings in a growth medium deficient in magnesium. The seedlings were left to grow under carefully controlled conditions.

Grade 6-7

a) Suggest why the scientist grew some of the seedlings in a growth medium containing a complete supply of minerals.

....

[1]

b) At the end of the investigation, the seedlings grown without magnesium had yellow leaves. The seedlings grown in a complete supply of minerals did not. Suggest why the magnesium-deficient plants had yellow leaves.

....

....

[1]

c) At the end of the investigation, the scientist measured the total dry mass of each group of plants. His results are shown in the graph to the right.

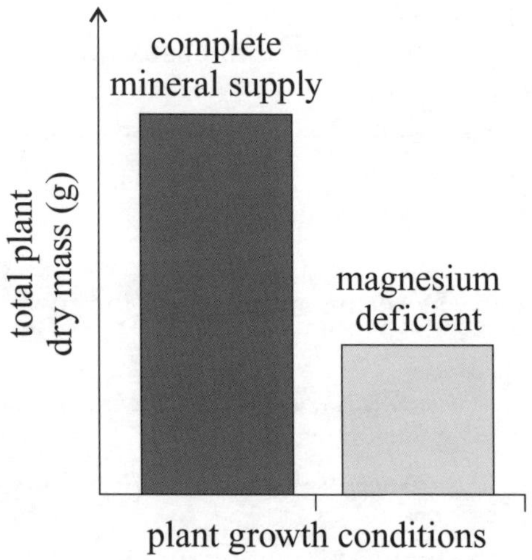

i) Describe the results shown in the graph.

....

....

....

[1]

ii) Suggest a possible explanation for the scientist's results.

....

....

....

....

[3]

[Total 6 marks]

Score:

8

Section 3 — Plant Nutrition and Transport

Transport in Plants

1 Aphids are insects that feed on plant sap. Sap is the name given to the liquids carried around a plant in transport vessels. It contains nutrients, such as sucrose. *(Grade 4-6)*

Which of the following statements about the sucrose-containing sap is correct?

☐ **A** The sap also contains amino acids and is transported in xylem vessels.

☐ **B** The sap also contains mineral ions and is transported in xylem vessels.

☐ **C** The sap also contains amino acids and is transported in phloem vessels.

☐ **D** The sap also contains mineral ions and is transported in phloem vessels.

[Total 1 mark]

2 Plants absorb water and mineral ions through their root hair cells. *(Grade 6-7)*

a) Name and describe the process by which water is drawn into a root hair cell from the soil.

....

....

....

[2]

b) Describe how root hair cells are adapted for absorbing lots of water from the soil.

....

[1]

[Total 3 marks]

3 Explain why small, unicellular organisms do not need a transport system, but large, multicellular organisms (such as plants) do. *(Grade 6-7)*

....

....

....

....

....

....

....

[Total 4 marks]

Paper 2

Exam Practice Tip

<u>F</u>ood <u>f</u>lows through the <u>ph</u>loem. It can be tricky to remember which is which when thinking of xylem and phloem. They're both pretty similar and have weird names. If there are facts you can't remember, it can be helpful to come up with phrases or rhymes which help to get them stuck in your head — no matter how silly.

Score

☐

8

Transpiration

1   A scientist measured the rate of transpiration in two plants over 48 hours.
The results are shown in the graph.

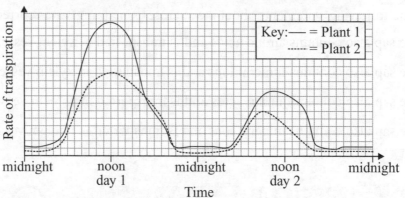

Key: —— = Plant 1
- - - - = Plant 2

a) Define the term transpiration.

....

           [1]

b) At what time on **day 2** was the rate of transpiration highest for **plant 2**? ....

           [1]

c) The rate of transpiration for both plants was slower on **day 2** than on **day 1**.
Suggest and explain **one** reason for this.

....

....

           [2]

d) Explain why the rate of transpiration for both plants was very low at night.

....

....

           [2]

[Total 6 marks]

2   The water loss from a plant in a hot, dry day is shown on the graph.

a) On the same axes, sketch the graph you would expect for
the same plant on a cold, wet day.

           [1]

b) Explain how temperature affects the rate of transpiration
in plants.

....

....

....

           [1]

[Total 2 marks]

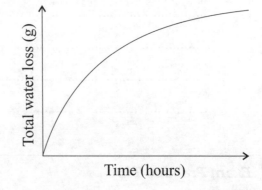

Score:

8

Paper 2

Measuring Transpiration

1 A student was investigating transpiration in basil plants under different conditions. She used twelve plants, three plants in each of the four different conditions. The plants were weighed before and after the experiment. She calculated the % loss in the mass per day and recorded her results in the table.

plant	in a room (% loss in mass)	next to a fan (% loss in mass)	by a lamp (% loss in mass)	next to a fan and by a lamp (% loss in mass)
1	5	8	10	13
2	5	9	11	15
3	4	11	9	13
mean	4.7	9.3		13.7

a) Calculate the mean % loss in plant mass for the three plants by a lamp.
Show your working.

mean % loss in mass .... %

[2]

b) Explain why the plants located next to a fan lost more mass than those in a still room.

....

....

....

....

....

[3]

c) Suggest why the student used three plants in each of the conditions shown.

....

[1]

d) Suggest how you could alter the student's experiment to investigate the effects of humidity on the rate of transpiration in basil plants.

....

....

[2]

[Total 8 marks]

Exam Practice Tip

Examiners love a good calculation question, especially one that involves having to calculate a mean, a percentage or a percentage change — so make sure you can do all three. And always, always show your working. You might pick up a mark for using the correct method, even if your final answer is wrong.

Score

8

Paper 2

Section 4 — Respiration and Gas Exchange

Respiration

1 Respiration is a process carried out by all living cells. It can take place aerobically or anaerobically.

Grade 4-6

a) State the purpose of respiration.

....

[1]

b) Give **two** differences between aerobic and anaerobic respiration.

1 ....

....

2 ....

....

[2]

c) Which of the following is the balanced symbol equation for aerobic respiration?

☐ **A** $C_6H_{12}O_6 + 6CO_2 \rightarrow 6O_2 + 6H_2O$ ☐ **C** $6O_2 + 6H_2O \rightarrow C_6H_{12}O_6 + 6CO_2$

☐ **B** $C_6H_{12}O_6 + 6O_2 \rightarrow 6CO_2 + 6H_2O$ ☐ **D** $6CO_2 + 6H_2O \rightarrow C_6H_{12}O_6 + 6O_2$

[1]

[Total 4 marks]

2 Anaerobic respiration is less efficient than aerobic respiration.

Grade 4-6

a) Suggest when a person would start to respire anaerobically.

....

[1]

b) Write the word equation for anaerobic respiration in humans.

....

[1]

c) Suggest **two** reasons why anaerobic respiration in humans is not efficient over long periods of time.

1 ....

2 ....

[2]

d) Plants can also respire anaerobically.
Name the **two** substances produced during anaerobic respiration in plants.

....

[2]

[Total 6 marks]

Score: ☐

10

Investigating Respiration

1 A student investigating respiration prepared a neutral solution of bromothymol blue indicator and added it to two test tubes. She put gauze platforms in both tubes and placed a living beetle in one tube and glass beads in the other (see below). She then sealed the tubes and left them for two hours.

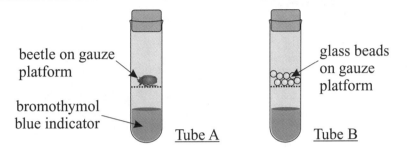

beetle on gauze platform

glass beads on gauze platform

bromothymol blue indicator

Tube A

Tube B

Bromothymol blue indicator is green in neutral solutions and yellow in acidic solutions. Carbon dioxide forms an acid when it dissolves in solution.

a) Describe and explain the appearance of each tube after the two hour period.

Tube A ....

....

Tube B ....

....

[4]

b) Explain why the student put glass beads into one of the tubes.

....

....

[1]

[Total 5 marks]

2 Describe an investigation to show that respiration produces a temperature change. Grade 6-7

....

....

....

....

....

....

....

....

[Total 6 marks]

Score: ☐

11

Gas Exchange — Flowering Plants

1 Plants exchange gases with the atmosphere. The diagram below shows a cross-section through part of a leaf, with arrows indicating the movement of two different gases during daylight hours.

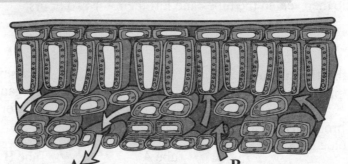

a) i) Suggest the gas that is most likely to be represented by each of the letters on the diagram.

   A ....   **B** ....

   [2]

   ii) Name the process by which gases move into and out of leaves.

   ....

   [1]

b) i) Which process in leaves produces oxygen as a waste product?

   ....

   [1]

   ii) Which process in leaves produces carbon dioxide as a waste product?

   ....

   [1]

   [Total 5 marks]

2 Leaves are adapted so that they are able to carry out efficient gas exchange.

Explain **three** ways in which a leaf is adapted for efficient gas exchange.

1 ....

....

2 ....

....

3 ....

....

   [Total 6 marks]

Section 4 — Respiration and Gas Exchange

3 The net exchange of carbon dioxide in plants changes throughout the day.

Explain the movement of carbon dioxide between the inside and outside of a leaf at night-time.

....

....

....

....

[Total 5 marks]

4 The graph below shows the oxygen and carbon dioxide exchanged by a plant.
The concentration of each gas was measured next to the leaves as light intensity increased.

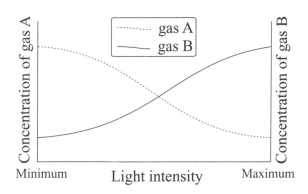

a) Which gas is oxygen and which is carbon dioxide? Explain your answers.

Gas A is ....

....

Gas B is ....

....

[4]

b) A student puts some pondweed in a tank and places it close to a window.
He then measures the concentration of carbon dioxide in the water over a 24 hour period.

At the time of the experiment, it was light between 6 am and 6 pm. Sketch the shape
of the graph you would expect the student's measurements to show on the axes below.

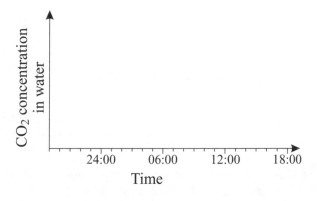

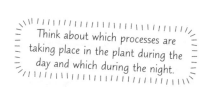

Think about which processes are taking place in the plant during the day and which during the night.

[2]

[Total 6 marks]

Section 4 — Respiration and Gas Exchange

5 A student has designed an experiment to investigate the effect of light intensity on net gas exchange in plants. He places healthy beech leaves into three tubes containing orange hydrogen-carbonate indicator and seals the tubes with rubber bungs. He prepares a fourth tube containing only indicator as a control.

In order to vary the amount of light reaching the three leaves, the student wraps tube **A** in gauze to block out some light, and tube **B** in foil to block out all light. He leaves tubes **C** and **D** (the control) unwrapped. His apparatus is shown below.

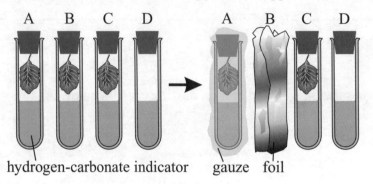

a) Suggest why the student sealed the tubes with rubber bungs.

....

[1]

b) Explain why the student included a control tube.

....

....

[1]

c) The student left the tubes near a bright light for two hours. After this time there was no change in the colour of the indicator solution in tube **D**. Explain the changes he saw in the indicator solution in the other three tubes, **A**, **B** and **C**, after the two hour period.

....

....

....

....

....

....

....

....

[6]

[Total 8 marks]

Exam Practice Tip

For Paper 2 you need to get your head around the balance of oxygen and carbon dioxide use and production by plants. The questions can look a bit tricky, but it all boils down to the fact that plants respire (use O_2, produce CO_2) all the time, but they can only photosynthesise (use CO_2, produce O_2) when it's light.

Score

☐

30

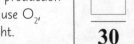

The Respiratory System and Ventilation

1 The respiratory system is found in the thorax. Grade 3-4

a) A diagram of the human thorax is shown below. Label the diaphragm and ribcage on the diagram.

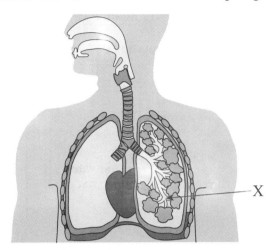

X

[2]

b) A structure of the respiratory system is labelled **X** in the diagram above. Name structure **X**.

....

[1]

c) Where in the respiratory system are the pleural membranes found?

....

[1]

d) Name the structures in the respiratory system where gas exchange takes place.

....

[1]

[Total 5 marks]

2 The statements below describe the events that take place when you breathe in. Put them in the correct order by writing the numbers **1** to **4** in the boxes, where **1** represents the first event. Grade 4-6

Event	Order
Pressure in lungs decreases	....
Intercostal muscles and diaphragm contract	....
Air enters the lungs	....
Thorax volume increases	....

[Total 3 marks]

Score:

8

Investigating Breathing

1   A student is investigating the presence of carbon dioxide in her breath.
Her experiment is set up as shown in the diagram below. As she inhales
through the mouthpiece, air is drawn in through boiling tube A.
As she exhales, the air bubbles through boiling tube B.

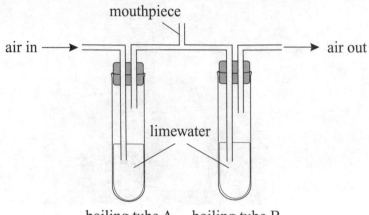

mouthpiece

air in →   → air out

limewater

boiling tube A   boiling tube B

The student inhales and exhales through the mouthpiece twenty times.
Explain any changes you would expect the student to observe.

....

....

....

[Total 2 marks]

2   Describe an investigation to find the effect of exercise on a person's breathing rate.   (Grade 6-7)

....

....

....

> The investigation you describe here can involve exercise of any type — the important thing is that you measure its effect on breathing rate.

....

....

....

....

....

[Total 6 marks]

Exam Practice Tip

When you're asked to describe an experiment, remember to talk about the things you would need to do to make sure that it's a fair test and that your results are valid and reliable. For example, remember to describe any variables that you need to control and make sure you say to repeat the experiment several times.

Score

[ ]

8

Gas Exchange — Humans

1 Gas exchange in humans occurs in the alveoli. (Grade 6-7)

a) Explain the exchange of oxygen between an alveolus and a capillary.

....

....

....

....

[3]

b) Explain **two** ways that alveoli are adapted for gas exchange.

1 ....

....

2 ....

....

[4]

[Total 7 marks]

2 The graph on the right shows how the percentage of smokers in the UK aged between 35 and 54 has changed since 1950. (Grade 7-9)

a) Describe the main trends shown by the graph.

....

....

[2]

b) Suggest **one** reason for the trend in the number of male smokers.

....

[1]

c) Explain **two** ways in which smoking can affect the lungs and circulatory system.

1 ....

....

2 ....

....

[4]

[Total 7 marks]

Score: ☐

14

Section 4 — Respiration and Gas Exchange

Functions of the Blood

1   Plasma is one of the main components of the blood. It is a pale yellow liquid which carries the other three main components of the blood and substances such as urea. **(Grade 4-6)**

a) Name the other **three** main components of the blood that are carried by the plasma.

....

[3]

b) Name **two** other substances that are transported in the plasma.

....

[2]

[Total 5 marks]

2   The cell shown below transports oxygen around the body. **(Grade 6-7)**

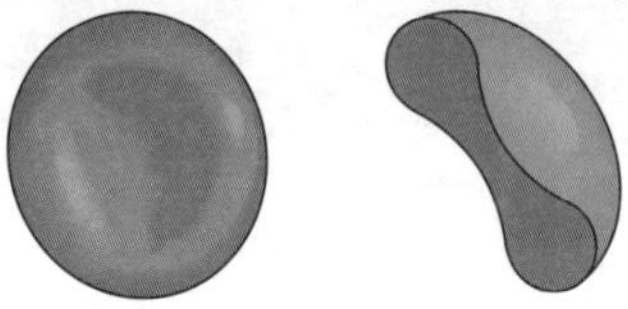

View from above   Cut through view

a) Explain how this cell's shape is adapted for transporting oxygen.

....

....

....

[2]

b) Explain **one** other way in which this cell is adapted for carrying oxygen.

....

....

[2]

[Total 4 marks]

3   Bernard-Soulier syndrome is a condition in which the blood fails to clot properly. **(Grade 6-7)**

a) Suggest which component of the blood is affected by Bernard-Soulier syndrome.

....

[1]

b) Explain why a normally minor injury such as a paper cut could be more serious for a person with Bernard-Soulier syndrome.

....

....

....

....

[3]

[Total 4 marks]

Score: ☐

13

☹ ☐   ☺ ☐   ☺ ☐

White Blood Cells and Immunity

1   The human immune system fights pathogens using a number of different mechanisms.

   a) Describe the mechanism for destroying pathogens which is shown in the diagram below.

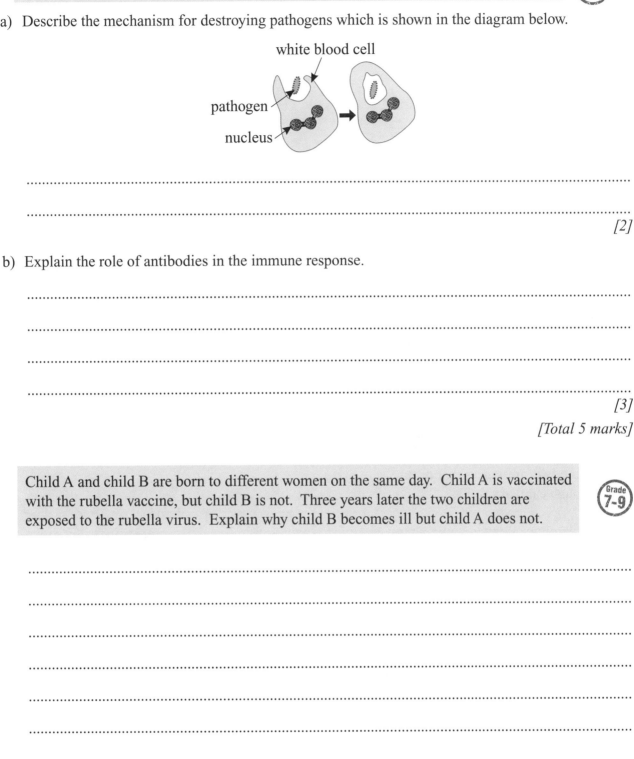

white blood cell

pathogen

nucleus

....

....

[2]

   b) Explain the role of antibodies in the immune response.

....

....

....

....

[3]

[Total 5 marks]

2   Child A and child B are born to different women on the same day. Child A is vaccinated with the rubella vaccine, but child B is not. Three years later the two children are exposed to the rubella virus. Explain why child B becomes ill but child A does not.

....

....

....

....

....

....

....

....

[Total 5 marks]

Score:

10

Section 5 — Blood and Organs

Blood Vessels

1 A student dissected out an artery and a vein from a piece of fresh meat. **Grade 6-7**

   a) Describe the roles of arteries and veins.

....

....

....

[2]

   b) Suggest **two** ways in which the student could tell which was the
artery and which was the vein when he was dissecting the meat.

....

....

[2]

   c) The student does an experiment and finds that one of the vessels is more elastic than the other.
Suggest which vessel is more elastic and explain how this is important for its function.

....

....

[2]
[Total 6 marks]

2 A diagram of a capillary is shown to the right. **Grade 6-7**

   a) Name **two** substances that diffuse
through capillary walls.

     1 ....

     2 ....

                       [2]

lumen

nucleus of cell

capillary

   b) Explain how the structure of a capillary is adapted for its function.

....

....

....

....

....

[6]
[Total 8 marks]

Exam Practice Tip

There are a fair few places in biology where you could be asked how the structure of something is related to its function. In these sorts of questions, don't just describe the function then rattle off what it looks like — make sure you clearly explain how each structural feature you mention helps with the function.

Score

14

Section 5 — Blood and Organs

The Heart

1   The diagram shows the human heart and four blood vessels, as seen from the front. The left ventricle has been labelled.

Grade 4-6

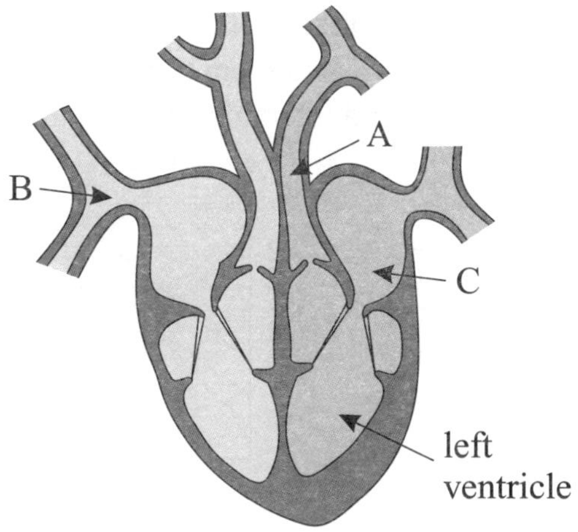

a) Name the parts labelled **A**, **B** and **C**.

A ....

B ....

C ....

[3]

b) Describe the function of the ventricles.

....

[1]

c) Describe the function of the valves in the heart.

....

[1]

d) Name the vessel which carries blood from the lungs to the heart.

....

[1]

[Total 6 marks]

2   Humans have a double circulatory system. This means that the heart pumps deoxygenated blood to the lungs in one circuit, and oxygenated blood to the body in another circuit.

Grade 6-7

a) Explain why the wall of the left ventricle is thicker than the wall of the right ventricle.

....

....

....

....

[4]

b) Describe how deoxygenated blood from the body passes through the heart to reach the lungs.

....

....

....

....

....

[4]

[Total 8 marks]

3 A student conducted an experiment to find out which of his friends has the shortest 'recovery time'.

Recovery time is how long it takes the heart rate to return to normal after exercise.
In separate tests, the student measured the heart rate of three friends by taking their pulses.
He then asked them to run for 2 minutes, after which he measured their heart rate at
15 second intervals until it returned to normal. His results are shown below.

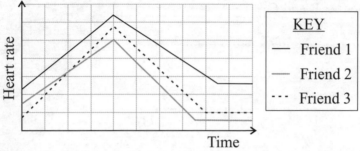

a) Which of the student's friends had the shortest recovery time? ....

[1]

b) Suggest **two** things the student should do to ensure that the test is fair.

1 ....

2 ....

[2]

c) The heart rate increases during exercise so that more oxygen is transported around the body.
Suggest why the body requires more oxygen during exercise.

....

....

[2]

[Total 5 marks]

4 A dog barks at a cat, causing the cat's heart rate to increase from 145 beats per minute to 170 beats per minute.

a) Explain the process which caused the cat's heart rate to increase.

....

....

....

....

....

[3]

b) Suggest how an increased heart rate prepares the cat for action.

....

[1]

[Total 4 marks]

Score: ⬜

23

Section 5 — Blood and Organs

Circulation and Coronary Heart Disease

1   The diagram shows the circulation system
     with some structures labelled A to H.
     Complete the table by writing in the
     letter that represents each structure.
     The first one has been done for you.

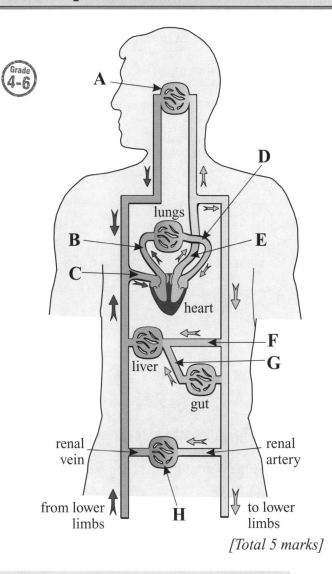

Structure	Letter
pulmonary artery	B
hepatic artery	....
vena cava	....
kidneys	....
aorta	....
hepatic portal vein	....

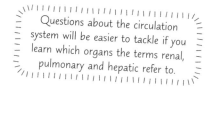

Questions about the circulation
system will be easier to tackle if you
learn which organs the terms renal,
pulmonary and hepatic refer to.

[Total 5 marks]

2   Doctors were assessing the heart of a patient who had recently suffered from a heart attack.
     They noticed that one of the main arteries supplying the heart muscle was narrowed.

a)   The patient is a smoker. Explain **one** way that smoking
     may have contributed to the narrowing of the artery.

     ....

     ....

                                                                                                                          [2]

b)   The patient is advised to stop smoking. Give **two** other pieces
     of lifestyle advice the doctors are likely to give to the patient.

     1 ....

     2 ....

                                                                                                                          [2]

[Total 4 marks]

Score: ☐

9

Excretion — The Kidneys

1 The kidneys are excretion organs which make up part of the urinary system. **Grade 4-6**

a) Name **one** other organ of the human body that's involved in the excretion of waste substances.

....
[1]

b) On the diagram below, label the **kidney**, **urethra** and **ureter**.

[3]

[Total 4 marks]

2 Ultrafiltration in the kidneys results in the production of glomerular filtrate. **Grade 6-7**

a) Name the part of the nephron where ultrafiltration occurs.

....
[1]

b) i) Describe how glomerular filtrate is produced in the body.

....

....

....

....
[3]

ii) The substances below are all involved in the process of ultrafiltration.

1. glucose
2. urea
3. proteins

Which of these substances are present in the glomerular filtrate?

☐ **A** 1 only   ☐ **B** 2 only   ☐ **C** 1 and 2 only   ☐ **D** 2 and 3 only

[1]

[Total 5 marks]

Score: ☐

9

Section 5 — Blood and Organs

Osmoregulation — The Kidneys

1 The kidneys play a key role in osmoregulation. **Grade 4-6**

a) What is meant by the term **osmoregulation**?

....

....

[1]

b) Name the fluid in which excess water is removed from the body.

....

[1]

c) i) Which of the following hormones controls the reabsorption of water in the kidneys?

    ☐ **A** oestrogen

    ☐ **B** ADH

    ☐ **C** adrenaline

    ☐ **D** insulin

[1]

ii) Name the part of the brain where this hormone is released.

....

[1]

[Total 4 marks]

2 A runner went for a 10 mile run on a warm day. When she got home she noticed that her urine was darker in colour than normal. Explain why the runner produced darker coloured urine. In your answer, refer to the functioning of the kidneys. **Grade 7-9**

....

....

....

....

....

....

....

....

[Total 6 marks]

Exam Practice Tip

Osmoregulation works by a negative feedback mechanism. This just means that if the body's water content goes too far in one direction, a mechanism is triggered to bring it back in the other direction.
Just make sure you remember which way round it works: less water results in more hormone secretion.

Score

☐

10

Section 5 — Blood and Organs

The Nervous System and Responding to Stimuli

1   Animals are able to detect changes in their environment.   Grade
     These changes are known as stimuli.   4-6

   a) Suggest why it's important for animals to be able to detect changes in their external environment.

      ....
                                                                                                              [1]

   b) Name the cells in the sense organs that detect stimuli.

      ....
                                                                                                              [1]

   c) Suggest what the stimulus, sense organ and effectors are in this scenario:

                When a hungry animal sees a source of food, it moves towards it.

      Stimulus ....

      Sense organ ....

      Effectors ....
                                                                                                              [3]

   d) The nervous system coordinates responses to stimuli.
      Name the other communication system in the body that coordinates responses to stimuli.

      ....
                                                                                                              [1]
                                                                                              [Total 6 marks]

2   The central nervous system coordinates responses   Grade
     to information it receives from the body.   4-6

   a) Name the **two** parts of the body which make up the central nervous system.

      1 ....

      2 ....
                                                                                                              [2]

   b) Name the type of neurone that carries information
      from the sense organs to the central nervous system.

      ....
                                                                                                              [1]

   c) Explain why the central nervous system produces very rapid responses to stimuli.

      ....
                                                                                                              [1]
                                                                                              [Total 4 marks]

3 Two scientists investigated how sensitive different parts of the body are to pressure.

The scientists used a cork with two pins mounted in it, spaced at a distance of 0.5 cm. Ten volunteers participated in the investigation. They were blindfolded and the pins were touched against different parts of their body. They reported 'yes' or 'no' when asked if they could feel the two individual pins. Their results are shown below.

Area of body tested	Number of volunteers that reported 'yes'
sole of foot	2
knee	3
fingertip	10
back of hand	5
lip	9

a) The scientists concluded that the fingertips are the part of the body with the most pressure receptors. Evaluate this conclusion.

A pressure receptor is a sensory receptor that detects touch (pressure).

....

....

....

[2]

b) One volunteer felt uncomfortable when the pins were placed against her lip, so she moved her head back. Explain how information was passed from her lip to the effectors in this coordinated response.

....

....

....

....

....

[4]

c) The two scientists took it in turn to test the volunteers. Explain how this affects the validity of the experiment.

....

....

[2]

d) Suggest why a man with a damaged spinal cord might not be able to feel the pins at all if they were placed against his knee.

....

....

[1]

[Total 9 marks]

Score: ☐

19

 ☐   ☐   ☐

Section 6 — Coordination and Response

Reflexes

1 Humans have many different reflexes. (Grade 3-4)

a) Which of the following sentences is correct?

☐ **A** Reflex reactions are slow and under conscious control.

☐ **B** Reflex reactions are slow and automatic.

☐ **C** Reflex reactions are rapid and automatic.

☐ **D** Reflex reactions are rapid and under conscious control.

[1]

b) Suggest **one** reason why reflex reactions are useful.

....

[1]

[Total 2 marks]

2 A man picked up a plate in the kitchen without realising it was hot, then immediately dropped it. The diagram below shows the reflex arc for this incident. (Grade 4-6)

spinal cord — X — receptor in skin — Y — muscle — Z

a) Name the **three** types of neurone labelled **X**, **Y** and **Z**.

X ....

Y ....

Z ....

[3]

b) State what the effectors are in this reflex arc and describe their response.

....

....

[2]

[Total 5 marks]

Exam Practice Tip

The pathway that nerve impulses take in a reflex arc is always the same — receptor, sensory neurone, relay neurone (in the spinal cord or an unconscious part of the brain), motor neurone, effector. Learn this pathway and then you'll be able to tackle any exam question on reflexes, even if it's a reflex you've not learnt.

Score

☐

7

Section 6 — Coordination and Response

The Eye

1 The diagram below shows a cross-section through the eye. _Grade 4-6_

a) Name the parts labelled:

A .... B ....

[2]

b) Describe the function of the iris.

....

....

[1]

iris

retina

[Total 3 marks]

2 The eye adjusts to different light levels. The diagrams on the right show the eye in two different light conditions. _Grade 6-7_

A B

a) Which diagram, **A** or **B**, shows the eye in bright light? Explain your answer.

....

....

[2]

b) The response of the eye to bright light is a reflex.
Suggest why it is an advantage to have this type of response controlling the action of the eye.

....

....

[2]

[Total 4 marks]

3 The eye adjusts its shape slightly to focus light. _Grade 6-7_

a) Describe how the eye adjusts to focus on distant objects.

....

....

....

[3]

b) Presbyopia is a condition in which the lens of the eye becomes less elastic and isn't easily able to form a rounded shape. Suggest how having presbyopia will affect a person's vision.

....

....

....

....

[2] **Score:**

[Total 5 marks] **12**

Hormones

1 Hormones are produced in glands and control many different processes in the body.

a) Complete the table below to show the name, source and effect(s) of three different hormones.

Hormone	Source	Effect(s)
Oestrogen	....	Controls the menstrual cycle and promotes female secondary sexual characteristics.
....	Adrenal glands	Increases heart rate, blood flow to muscles and blood sugar level.
Progesterone	Ovaries	....

[3]

b) i) Name the main male sex hormone and state its source.

....

[2]

ii) Describe the role and effect of the hormone insulin.

....

....

[2]

c) Describe the physical change that the hormone ADH brings about.

....

[1]

[Total 8 marks]

2 Responses to stimuli can be either nervous or hormonal.

Describe the differences between responses brought about by hormones and those brought about by the nervous system.

....

....

....

....

....

[Total 4 marks]

Exam Practice Tip

Hormones crop up a lot in biology, so there's a good chance you'll be asked about one of the hormones on this page — make sure you know the source, role and effect of each. Being able to recall straightforward facts like these can net you some pretty easy marks in the exam, so it's worth taking the time to learn them well.

Score

[ ]

12

Homeostasis

1 A cyclist goes for a bike ride. It is a hot day and he has to work hard on some steep hills. Homeostasis helps to regulate the water content in his body. **Grade 4-6**

a) What is meant by the term **homeostasis**?

....

[1]

b) i) Describe **two** ways in which the cyclist's body loses water while he is cycling.

1 ....

2 ....

[2]

ii) When the cyclist returns home, he notices that his urine is dark in colour. Suggest why.

....

....

[2]

c) The cyclist does exactly the same bike ride the following day, but notices afterwards that his urine is not as dark in colour this time. Suggest **one** possible reason for this.

....

[1]

[Total 6 marks]

2 Human core body temperature is around 37 °C. **Grade 6-7**

a) Explain why human body temperature needs to be kept at around 37 °C.

....

....

[1]

b) A woman is on holiday in Norway. It is –5 °C and she is feeling cold.
Explain how the woman's nervous system responds to the low temperature
in order to maintain a safe body temperature.

....

....

....

....

....

[3]

[Total 4 marks]

Score: ▢

10

More on Homeostasis

1   Changes in the skin are an important part of temperature regulation. The diagram on the right shows a cross-section through the skin of a person who is cold.

hairs

sweat gland

blood vessels

a) In the diagram, blood vessels close to the surface of the skin have narrowed.

    i) Give the scientific name for this process.

    ....

                       [1]

    ii) Explain why the blood vessels have narrowed.

    ....

    ....

                       [2]

b) Explain the response of a sweat gland when a person is cold.

    ....

    ....

                       [2]

              [Total 5 marks]

2   Temperatures in a sauna can reach up to 100 °C.

a) Explain why a person using a sauna may be advised to drink water regularly.

    ....

    ....

                       [2]

b) Explain **two** ways that a person's body would respond to being in a sauna.

    ....

    ....

    ....

    ....

    ....

                       [6]

              [Total 8 marks]

Score:

13

Responses in Plants

1 A student placed some germinating beans on the surface of some damp soil and left them for five days. The appearance of the beans before and after the five day period is shown below.

Grade 4-6

> Germination is when a plant starts to grow from a seed.

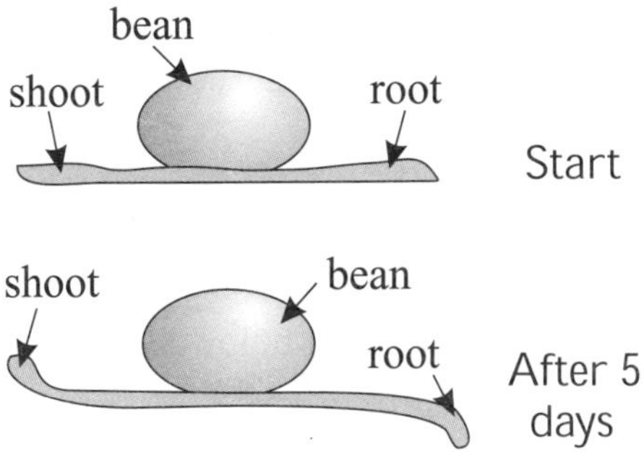

a) i) What is meant by the term **negative geotropism**?

....

....
[1]

ii) Which part of the seedling is demonstrating negative geotropism after five days?

....
[1]

b) i) After the five day period, the student turned the seeds upside down, as shown to the right. State the direction in which the root will grow after the seed is turned upside down.

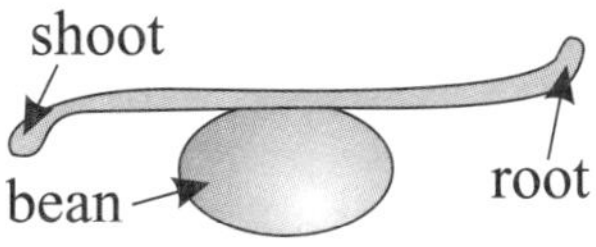

....
[1]

ii) Which of the following explains this direction of root growth?

☐ **A** Auxin builds up on the upper side of the root, inhibiting growth of upper cells.

☐ **B** Auxin builds up on the upper side of the root, inhibiting growth of lower cells.

☐ **C** Auxin builds up on the lower side of the root, inhibiting growth of upper cells.

☐ **D** Auxin builds up on the lower side of the root, inhibiting growth of lower cells.

[1]
[Total 4 marks]

2 A plant is growing behind a building in the shade. As it grows, it bends around the corner of the building towards the sunlight.

Grade 6-7

a) Explain the importance of the growth of the plant towards the sunlight.

....

....
[1]

b) Explain how the plant grows towards the sunlight.

....

....

....

....
[3]
[Total 4 marks]

Section 6 — Coordination and Response

3 The nutrients a plant needs to survive are often found deep in the soil. *(Grade 6-7)*

Suggest how positive geotropism helps a plant to survive.

....

....

....

[Total 3 marks]

4 An investigation was done to find out how plant shoots respond to light.
Three plant shoots (**A**, **B** and **C**) were exposed to a light stimulus.
The diagram below shows the shape of each shoot before and after the experiment. *(Grade 7-9)*

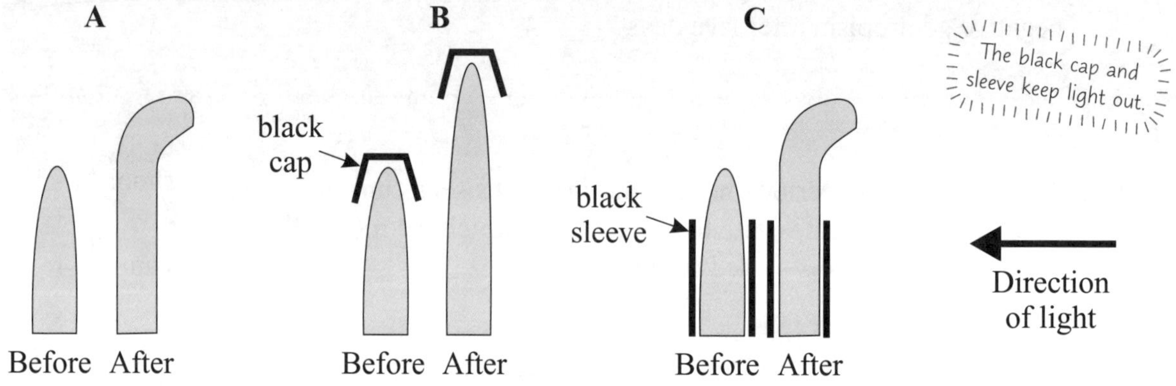

black cap

black sleeve

The black cap and sleeve keep light out.

Direction of light

A   B   C

Before After   Before After   Before After

a) Using the results of the experiment, suggest which part of the plant shoot is most sensitive to light.

....

[1]

b) Explain the growth of shoot **B** during the experiment.

....

....

....

[3]

c) Give **two** variables that should have been controlled in this experiment.

1 ....

2 ....

[2]

d) Suggest how the results of the experiment may have been different if the tips of
the shoots were removed at the start of the experiment. Explain your answer.

....

....

[2]

[Total 8 marks]

Score: ⬜

19

Section 6 — Coordination and Response

DNA, Genes and Chromosomes

1   DNA in plants and animals is found in the form of chromosomes.   *(Grade 4-6)*

a) Name the part of the cell where chromosomes are found.

....

[1]

b) i) The body cells of most mammals are **diploid**. Explain what this means.

....

[1]

ii) State the diploid number for humans. ....

[1]

c) Which of the following describes the structure of a DNA molecule?

☐   **A** One strand of bases coiled into a single helix.

☐   **B** One strand of amino acids coiled into a single helix

☐   **C** Two strands held together by base pairs in the shape of a double helix.

☐   **D** Two strands held together by amino acids in the shape of a double helix.

[1]

[Total 4 marks]

2   Genes are short sections of DNA.   *(Grade 6-7)*

a) Explain the relationship between genes and the characteristics of an organism.

....

....

[2]

b) Fur length in cats is controlled by a single gene.
A female cat gave birth to a litter of two kittens, shown on the
right. One kitten is long-haired and the other is short-haired.
Explain why the kittens show different characteristics.

Think about how a single gene is able to produce different characteristics.

....

....

....

....

....

[3]

[Total 5 marks]

Score: ☐

9

 ☐   ☐   ☐

Protein Synthesis

1 A gene in a species of flowering plant codes for a protein that determines flower colour. A sequence of bases in a section of this gene is shown below.

A T C C C G A A C T C G G C

What is the maximum number of amino acids that can be coded for by this gene?

☐ **A** 6	☐ **C** 4
☐ **B** 5	☐ **D** 3

[Total 1 mark]

2 To make a protein, the base sequence in the coding DNA of a gene is copied into mRNA.

a) Which of the following sets of bases are found in mRNA?

☐ **A** A, T, C, G	☐ **C** A, U, C, G
☐ **B** A, T, C, U	☐ **D** A, E, C, G

[1]

b) Which of the following is the name for a set of three bases in mRNA?

☐ **A** an amino acid	☐ **C** a gene
☐ **B** a codon	☐ **D** a variant

[1]

c) Name the part of the cell in which mRNA is made.

....

[1]

d) Name the process that ensures the mRNA produced is a complementary copy of the gene.

....

[1]

e) Describe the role of tRNA in protein synthesis.

....

[1]

f) Explain the purpose of mRNA.

....

....

[2]

[Total 7 marks]

3 Two different proteins found in the human body are shown below on the right. Collagen is a structural protein. It supports structures such as muscle tendons. Haemoglobin is a transport protein. It transports oxygen around the body.

Grade 7-9

With reference to genes, explain how it is possible for these two proteins to have such different functions.

collagen   haemoglobin

....

....

....

....

[Total 4 marks]

4 The diagram below shows a section of DNA containing coding and non-coding regions.

Grade 7-9

Non-coding DNA   Gene (coding DNA)   Non-coding DNA

Explain how a protein would be produced from this section of DNA in a cell.

....

....

....

....

....

....

....

....

....

....

....

....

....

[Total 6 marks]

Paper 2 (side margin)

Exam Practice Tip

Protein synthesis is a tricky topic and there's an awful lot to remember here. The best way to learn it is to break it down into stages (transcription and translation) and then go over the steps involved in each stage in order, until you've grasped them. And remember, mRNA is the messenger and tRNA transfers amino acids.

Score

18

Section 7 — Reproduction and Inheritance

Asexual Reproduction and Mitosis

1 Some species of starfish can produce offspring through a process called fission. In this process, the parent's body splits into two parts that undergo cell division by mitosis to develop into mature, complete organisms.

Grade 4-6

a) Give the term that is used to describe this form of reproduction.

....
[1]

b) Suggest how the chromosomes in the offspring will compare to those of the parent starfish.

....
[1]

c) Other than reproduction, suggest **one** function of mitosis in starfish.

....
[1]

[Total 3 marks]

2 The graph shows how the amount of DNA per cell changes as a cell undergoes two cell divisions by mitosis. Point **C** is the time when the chromosomes first become visible in the new cells.

Grade 7-9

a) Describe what is happening to the DNA during stage **A**. Suggest why this needs to happen.

....

....

....
[2]

b) Suggest what happens at time **B**.

....
[1]

c) State how many cells there will be after the first cell division.

....
[1]

[Total 4 marks]

Score:

7

Sexual Reproduction and Meiosis

1   Mosquitoes have three pairs of chromosomes in their body cells. **Cell A**, shown to the right, is a mosquito cell which is about to divide by meiosis.

Grade 6-7

cell A

a)   i) State the haploid number of a cell produced when cell A undergoes meiosis.

....

[1]

ii) State the number of cells that will be produced in total when cell A undergoes meiosis.

....

[1]

b) Explain how the processes of meiosis and fertilisation lead to genetic variation in the mosquito's offspring.

....

....

....

....

[3]

[Total 5 marks]

2   The diagram below shows two cells. The cell on the left has duplicated DNA and is about to undergo meiosis.

Grade 6-7

meiosis →

a) In the cell on the right, sketch the number of chromosomes that would be present after meiosis in one of the daughter cells.

[1]

b) Explain why meiosis is necessary for sexual reproduction.

....

....

....

[3]

[Total 4 marks]

Exam Practice Tip

There are a lot of terms to remember here. If you get a question on cell division, be sure to read it carefully — 'meiosis' and 'mitosis' are very similar words. If in doubt, remember that bacteria <u>might</u> reproduce by <u>mi</u>tosis, but <u>my</u> children will be produced by <u>me</u>iosis. It sounds a bit silly, but it might be useful in the exam.

Score

9

Sexual Reproduction in Plants

1 Flowering plants contain both male and female organs. They are able to reproduce sexually via pollination. **Grade 4-6**

   a) Describe what happens during pollination.

     ....

     ....

     [3]

   b) Cross-pollination is the term used to describe sexual reproduction involving two different plants. Suggest what is meant by the term **self-pollination**.

     ....

     [1]

     [Total 4 marks]

2 The diagram below shows cross-sections through two flowers. **Grade 6-7**

A   B

X   Y

   a) Look at flower **A**. State the name and function of the structures labelled **X** and **Y**.

     X ....

     Y ....

     [4]

   b) Explain which flower, **A** or **B**, is better adapted for wind pollination.

     ....

     ....

     [2]

   c) Explain **two** ways in which flowers can be adapted for pollination by insects.

     1 ....

     2 ....

     [2]

     [Total 8 marks]

Score:

12

Fertilisation and Germination in Plants

1 Fertilisation in plants results in the formation of a seed. **Grade 6-7**

a) Describe how a seed forms when a pollen grain from one plant lands on the stigma of another plant.

....

....

....

....

....

....

[5]

b) Describe how a germinating seed obtains energy for growth.

....

[1]

[Total 6 marks]

2 A student set up a controlled experiment to investigate the conditions needed for germination. **Grade 7-9**

She placed moist cotton wool and soaked alfalfa seeds in two large sealed flasks.

Flask **A** contained sodium pyrogallate solution, which absorbs oxygen from the air.
Flask **B** contained sodium hydroxide solution, which absorbs carbon dioxide from the air.

After 24 hours, she found that the seeds had germinated in flask **B** only.

(Diagram labels: moist cotton wool and alfalfa seeds; gauze; sodium pyrogallate solution; sodium hydroxide solution; flasks A and B)

a) Explain why germination did not occur in flask **A**.

....

....

[2]

b) The student left flask B for a further 6 days. She observed that the seedlings produced green leaves after 4 days, but then showed no further growth despite still being alive. Suggest why the seedlings in flask **B** stopped growing after they had produced green leaves.

....

....

....

....

....

[3] **Score:** ☐

[Total 5 marks] **11**

 ☐   ☐   ☐

PRACTICAL Investigating Seed Germination

1   A student is investigating how water, oxygen and temperature affect germination.

His experiment is set up as shown in the diagram below.

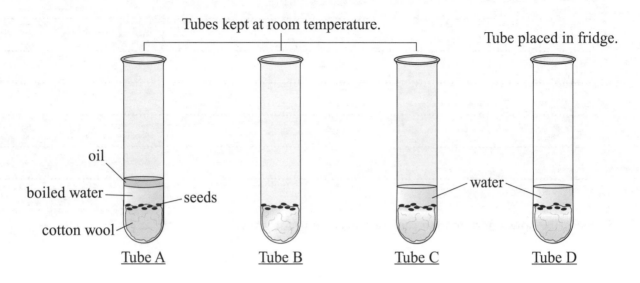

Tubes kept at room temperature.

Tube placed in fridge.

oil

boiled water — seeds

cotton wool

water

Tube A   Tube B   Tube C   Tube D

The student makes sure that all other variables are controlled and leaves the tubes for five days.

a) Explain which tube is the control in this experiment.

....

....

[1]

b) Explain what the student will observe in tubes **A**, **B** and **C**.

Tube A ....

....

Tube B ....

....

Tube C ....

....

[6]

c) The student observes that the low temperature prevented the seeds in tube **D** from germinating.
Suggest why a low temperature prevents germination.

....

[1]

[Total 8 marks]

Exam Practice Tip

In some exam questions, there might be an investigation using a different method to the one you've used in class. But don't let that throw you off if you're asked to predict the results of an experiment. If you've learnt the effects of changing different variables, you can apply that knowledge to any question about it.

Score

8

Asexual Reproduction in Plants

1   Some plants, such as daffodils and strawberry plants, can reproduce asexually.   (Grade 6-7)

   a) Strawberry plants reproduce asexually using runners.
Explain what is meant by the term **runners** and describe how they allow plants to reproduce.

....

....

....

[2]

   b) A strawberry plant is genetically susceptible to a particular virus. Explain why any offspring
the plant produces through asexual reproduction will also be susceptible to the virus.

....

....

[1]

[Total 3 marks]

2   A scientist has bred a high yield grapevine that seems to be
resistant to the grapevine chrome mosaic virus. She wants to
clone the vine to produce new plants to continue her research.   (Grade 6-7)

   a) Suggest **one** reason why the scientist wants to clone the
plants rather than allow them to reproduce sexually.

....

....

....

[2]

   b) Give **one** artificial method that the scientist could use to clone the grapevine.

....

[1]

[Total 3 marks]

Score:

6

Human Reproductive Systems

1 The diagram below shows the male reproductive system. **Grade 3-4**

a) Name the structures labelled **X** and **Y**.

X ....

Y ....
[2]

b) The structure labelled **Z** is a gland.
State its function.

....

....
[1]

c) Add an arrow to the diagram to show where sperm cells are produced.
[1]

[Total 4 marks]

2 Sex hormones begin to be produced during puberty. **Grade 4-6**

a) Give **two** secondary sexual characteristics caused by the male sex hormone, testosterone.

1 ....

2 ....
[2]

b) i) Name the female sex hormone. ....
[1]

ii) Give **one** secondary sexual characteristic that this hormone causes in women.

....
[1]

[Total 4 marks]

3 Give the name and function of **three** structures in the female reproductive system. **Grade 6-7**

1 ....

....

2 ....

....

3 ....

....

[Total 6 marks]

Score:

14

Section 7 — Reproduction and Inheritance

The Menstrual Cycle and Pregnancy

1 Which of the following hormones is responsible for stimulating egg maturation?

Grade 3-4

☐ **A** oestrogen ☐ **B** progesterone ☐ **C** LH ☐ **D** FSH

[Total 1 mark]

2 The diagram to the right shows the uterus during pregnancy.

Grade 4-6

wall of uterus — amnion
umbilical cord — developing baby (fetus)
placenta — amniotic fluid

Describe the role of the following features shown in the diagram:

a) the placenta

....

....

[1]

b) the amniotic fluid

....

[1]

[Total 2 marks]

3 The diagram shows the levels of oestrogen and progesterone over a 28 day menstrual cycle.

Grade 6-7

egg released

Level of hormone

A

B

day 14

Time

a) State which curve, **A** or **B**, represents oestrogen. Explain your answer.

....

....

[1]

b) During which part of the cycle is the lining of the uterus thickest? Explain your answer.

....

....

[2]

[Total 3 marks]

Score: ☐

6

Genetic Diagrams

1 An individual carries a recessive allele, **b**, for red hair and a dominant allele, **B**, for brown hair.

Grade 4-6

a) Give the individual's phenotype.

....

[1]

b) The individual's genotype is **Bb**. Give the term used to describe this genotype.

....

[1]

[Total 2 marks]

2 Fruit flies usually have red eyes. However, there are a small number of white-eyed fruit flies. Having white eyes is a recessive characteristic.

Grade 6-7

Two fruit flies with red eyes have the heterozygous genotype for this characteristic. They are crossed to produce offspring.

a) Complete the genetic diagram below to show the genotypes of the parent flies, the genotypes of the parents' gametes and the genotypes and phenotypes of the possible offspring.

Use **R** to represent the dominant allele and **r** to represent the recessive allele.

Genotypes of parents:

Genotypes of gametes:

Genotypes of offspring:

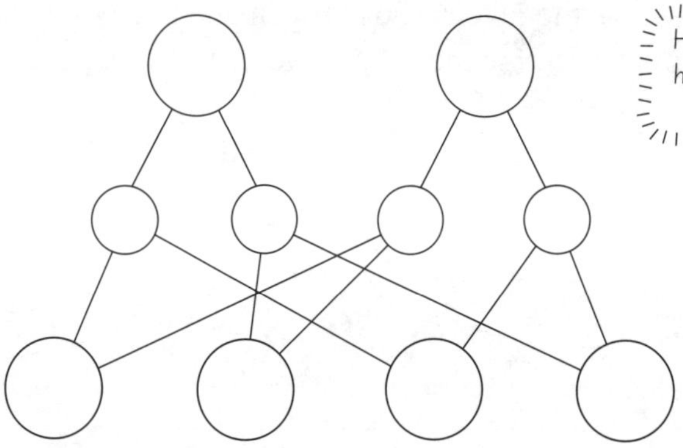

Phenotypes of offspring:

Heterozygous individuals have two different alleles for a particular gene.

[3]

b) i) State the probability that one of the fruit flies' offspring will have white eyes.

....

[1]

ii) The fruit flies have 60 offspring. Calculate how many of the offspring are likely to have red eyes. Show your working.

....

[2]

[Total 6 marks]

Section 7 — Reproduction and Inheritance

3 Albinism is a condition characterised by a lack of pigment in the hair and skin. It is caused by the recessive allele **a**. The dominant allele **A** results in normal pigmentation.

Grade 7-9

a) State the possible genotypes of a rabbit that shows no symptoms of albinism.

....
[1]

A rabbit with albinism mated with a rabbit that showed no symptoms of the condition. They produced 12 offspring, 7 of which had albinism.

b) Calculate the percentage of offspring with albinism. Show your working.

.... %
[2]

c) i) Deduce the genotypes of the parent rabbits. Use a genetic diagram to show the parents' genotypes, the genotypes of their gametes, and the possible genotypes and phenotypes of the offspring.

If you're not told how to construct your genetic diagram, you can draw it however you like, as long as it's clear.

[3]

ii) Using your genetic diagram, give the percentage of offspring that are likely to have albinism.

....
[1]

iii) Explain why the percentage of offspring with albinism you calculated in part b) is not the same as that suggested by the genetic diagram.

....

....
[1]

[Total 8 marks]

Exam Practice Tip

When you draw a genetic diagram, don't be tempted to take a short cut and miss out any stages — always show the parents' genotypes, the gametes' genotypes and the genotypes and phenotypes of the offspring. The question might prompt you to do this, but it's good practice to get into the habit now.

Score

16

Section 7 — Reproduction and Inheritance

More Genetic Diagrams

1 Treacher Collins syndrome is characterised by deformed or missing bones in the face.
It is thought to be transmitted by the dominant allele **T**.
Severe forms of the syndrome can result in life-threatening breathing difficulties.

A man with mild symptoms of Treacher Collins syndrome is heterozygous for the gene.
His wife does not have the syndrome. Before deciding whether to have children, the couple
wish to know what the probability is of their child inheriting the condition.

a) Complete the Punnett square to show the genotypes and gametes of the couple, and the possible
genotypes and phenotypes of their children. Use **T** and **t** to represent the alleles.

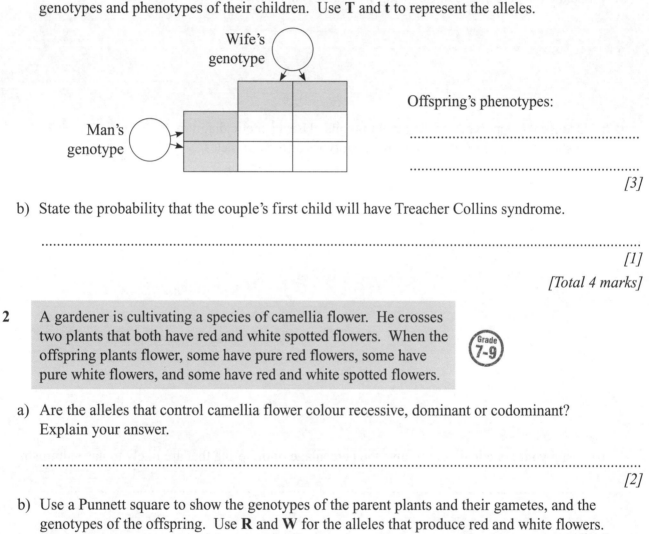

Offspring's phenotypes:

....

....

[3]

b) State the probability that the couple's first child will have Treacher Collins syndrome.

....

[1]

[Total 4 marks]

2 A gardener is cultivating a species of camellia flower. He crosses
two plants that both have red and white spotted flowers. When the
offspring plants flower, some have pure red flowers, some have
pure white flowers, and some have red and white spotted flowers.

(Grade 7-9)

a) Are the alleles that control camellia flower colour recessive, dominant or codominant?
Explain your answer.

....

[2]

b) Use a Punnett square to show the genotypes of the parent plants and their gametes, and the
genotypes of the offspring. Use **R** and **W** for the alleles that produce red and white flowers.

[3]

c) State the phenotypic ratio of the offspring produced by this cross.

red : spotted : white flowers .... : .... : ....

[1]

Score:

[Total 6 marks]

10

Section 7 — Reproduction and Inheritance

Family Pedigrees and Sex Determination

1 Polydactyly is a genetic disorder transmitted by the dominant allele **D**. The corresponding recessive allele is **d**. The family pedigree of a family with a history of polydactyly is shown below.

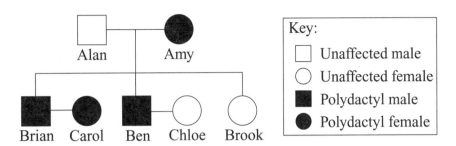

Using the information given above, state what Amy's genotype must be.
Explain your answer.

....

....

....

[Total 2 marks]

2 The family pedigree below shows a family with a history of cystic fibrosis. Cystic fibrosis is caused by the recessive allele **f**. Both Libby and Anne are pregnant. They don't yet know whether their babies have the disorder.

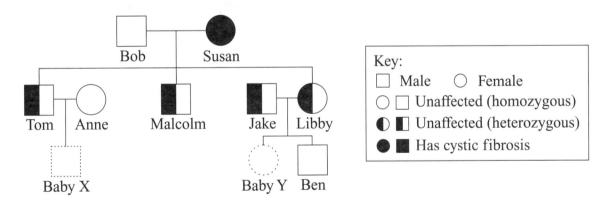

a) Using **F** and **f** to represent the alleles, state the genotypes of the following people:

Susan .... Anne .... Libby ....

[3]

b) Complete the table to show the probability of Baby X and Baby Y suffering from cystic fibrosis.

	Probability of cystic fibrosis
Baby X	
Baby Y	

[2]

[Total 5 marks]

3 In crickets of the *Orthoptera* order, there is only one sex chromosome, X. A cricket with two copies of the chromosome (XX) is female. A cricket with only one copy of the chromosome (X0) is male — '0' indicates the absence of a second chromosome.

a) Draw a genetic diagram to show the inheritance of sex chromosomes in crickets of the *Orthoptera* order, including the chromosomes of the gametes and offspring, and the sex of the offspring.

> Don't let the '0' in the 'X0' put you off here. Just treat it like another chromosome.

[3]

b) A female *Orthoptera* cricket lays 170 eggs that all hatch to produce offspring. Calculate how many of the offspring are likely to be male. Show your working.

....

[2]

[Total 5 marks]

4 Colour blindness in humans is caused by a recessive allele located on the X chromosome. It is more common in men because men carry only one X chromosome.

A man who is colour-blind has a child with a woman who does not have the recessive allele.

a) Draw a genetic diagram to show the sex chromosomes of the parents and the gametes they produce, the possible combinations of sex chromosomes in the offspring and the sex of the offspring.

[3]

> Think about which sex chromosome the boy inherits from his father.

b) The child is a boy. Explain why the boy will not be colour-blind.

....

....

[1]

c) State the probability that a daughter of this couple would be colour-blind. ....

[1]

[Total 5 marks]

Score: ☐

17

Section 7 — Reproduction and Inheritance

Variation

1 Helen and Stephanie are identical twins. (Grade 6-7)

a) Helen has brown hair and Stephanie has blonde hair.
   Are these likely to be the natural hair colours of both girls? Explain your answer.

   ....

   ....
   [2]

b) Helen weighs 7 kg more than Stephanie.
   Explain whether this is due to genes, environmental factors or both.

   ....

   ....

   ....
   [2]

c) Stephanie has a birthmark on her shoulder. Helen doesn't.
   State whether birthmarks are caused by genes and explain your answer.

   ....

   ....
   [1]
   [Total 5 marks]

2 A racehorse owner wants to produce a successful foal from one of his thoroughbred mares. He takes the mare to breed with a prize-winning stallion. (Grade 7-9)

Suggest whether or not the racehorse owner can confidently expect the foal to be a successful racehorse. Explain your answer.

....

....

....

....

....

....
[Total 4 marks]

Score: [ ]

9

Evolution and Natural Selection

1 The photograph shows an adult buff tip moth. The buff tip moth's appearance mimics a broken twig, making it well camouflaged. Explain how the moth might have evolved to look like this.

Grade 7-9

....

....

....

....

....

....

....

....

....

Think about how the appearance of the buff tip moth increases its chances of survival.

[Total 5 marks]

2 A population of finches on an island mainly eat seeds. The finches vary in the size of their beaks. Larger beaks are better for breaking apart larger seeds, whereas smaller beaks are better for picking up and eating smaller seeds. A storm kills off many of the plants that produce larger seeds.

Grade 7-9

Describe how evolution by natural selection may lead to a change in the beak size in the population of finches, following the storm.

....

....

....

....

....

....

....

....

....

....

[Total 6 marks]

Score:

11

73

Mutations and Antibiotic Resistance

1 Genetic variation in a population arises partly due to mutations. `Grade 4-6`

a) Describe what is meant by the term **mutation**.

....
[2]

b) Explain how mutations can increase variation in a species.

....

....

....
[3]

[Total 5 marks]

2 *Staphylococcus aureus* (SA) is a common bacterium that is found on the skin and mucous membranes. It can cause a range of infections. Some strains of SA have developed resistance to the antibiotic methicillin, and are known as methicillin-resistant *Staphylococcus aureus* (MRSA). `Grade 6-7`

a) Name the process that leads to the spread of antibiotic resistance in bacteria.

....
[1]

b) The statements below describe the different stages that led to *Staphylococcus aureus* becoming resistant to methicillin. Put them in the correct order by writing the numbers **1** to **4** in the boxes, where **1** represents the first stage.

Stage	Order
The gene for methicillin resistance became more common in the population over time.	....
Individual bacteria with the mutated genes were more likely to survive and reproduce in a host being treated with methicillin.	....
Random mutations in the DNA of *Staphylococcus aureus* led to it being less affected by methicillin.	....
The gene for methicillin resistance was passed on to lots of offspring, who also survived and reproduced.	....

[2]

[Total 3 marks]

Score:

9

Section 8 — Ecology and the Environment

Ecosystems and Biodiversity

1 The Amazon rainforest is the biggest tropical rainforest in the world. (Grade 4-6)

a) Scientists are concerned that deforestation and climate change will reduce the rainforest's biodiversity. What is meant by the term biodiversity?

....

....

[1]

b) The Amazon rainforest is a habitat for many different species. Describe what is meant by a habitat.

....

[1]

c) Which word can be used to describe all the different species living in a habitat?

☐ **A** population

☐ **B** community

☐ **C** ecosystem

☐ **D** distribution

[1]

[Total 3 marks]

2 Prickly acacia is a tree species native to many African and Asian countries. It was introduced to Australia many years ago. It has invaded large areas of land in the warmer parts of the country. The trees grow best in areas with a high average temperature and where there is plenty of water, such as along rivers or on flood plains where there is seasonal flooding. (Grade 6-7)

a) Australia experienced particularly high rainfall in the 1950s and 1970s. Suggest how the prickly acacia population in Australia may have changed during these periods. Explain your answer.

....

....

[2]

b) Global temperature is thought to be increasing. What may happen to the distribution of prickly acacia in Australia over the next few decades? Explain your answer.

....

....

[2]

c) When prickly acacia invades an area, it can negatively impact the populations of various grasses in that area. Suggest why this might be the case.

....

....

....

[1]

Score:

8

[Total 5 marks]

Using Quadrats

1   A group of students used a quadrat with an area of 0.5 m² to investigate the
    number of buttercups growing in a field. They counted the number of buttercups
    in the quadrat in ten randomly selected places. The table below shows their results.

Quadrat Number	Number of buttercups
1	15
2	13
3	16
4	23
5	26
6	23
7	13
8	12
9	16
10	13

a) i) Explain why it is important that the quadrats were randomly placed in the field.

    ....
                                                                                                                    [1]

    ii) Describe a method that could have been used to randomly place the quadrats.

    ....
                                                                                                                    [1]

b) Calculate the mean number of buttercups per 0.5 m² quadrat.

                                                    .... buttercups per 0.5 m²
                                                                                                                    [1]

c) The total area of the field was 1750 m².
    Estimate the number of buttercups in the whole of the field.

                                                    .... buttercups
                                                                                                                    [2]

d) Suggest how the accuracy of this estimate could be improved.

    ....
                                                                                                                    [1]
                                                                                                        [Total 6 marks]

2 Bill investigated the distribution of dandelions across a field next to a wood. A sketch Bill drew of the area is shown below.

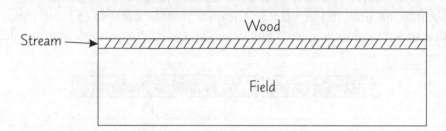

The following table shows the results of Bill's investigation.

Number of dandelions per m²	5	9	14	19	26
Distance from wood (m)	2	4	6	8	10

a) Describe how Bill could have used quadrats to obtain these results.

....

....

....

....

[4]

b) Describe the trend in Bill's results.

....

....

[1]

Bill wanted to see if the trend in the distribution of dandelions was due to varying light intensity across the area investigated. He measured the light intensity and found it decreased towards the wood. He concluded that the distribution of dandelions depended on the light intensity.

c) Explain why Bill's results are not valid.

....

> Valid results are reliable and come from an investigation that was designed to be a fair test.

....

[2]

d) Suggest another variable that could have affected the distribution of dandelions.

....

[1]

[Total 8 marks]

Exam Practice Tip

Make sure you can describe how a transect is used to gather data, and how this data can be used to estimate and study population size. It sounds obvious, but you should always check your answers to make sure they're sensible — if you only find a few daisies in a field, they won't have a very high percentage cover.

Score

14

Section 8 — Ecology and the Environment

Pyramids of Number, Biomass and Energy

1   A student is studying the following food chain on the beach.   (Grade 4-6)

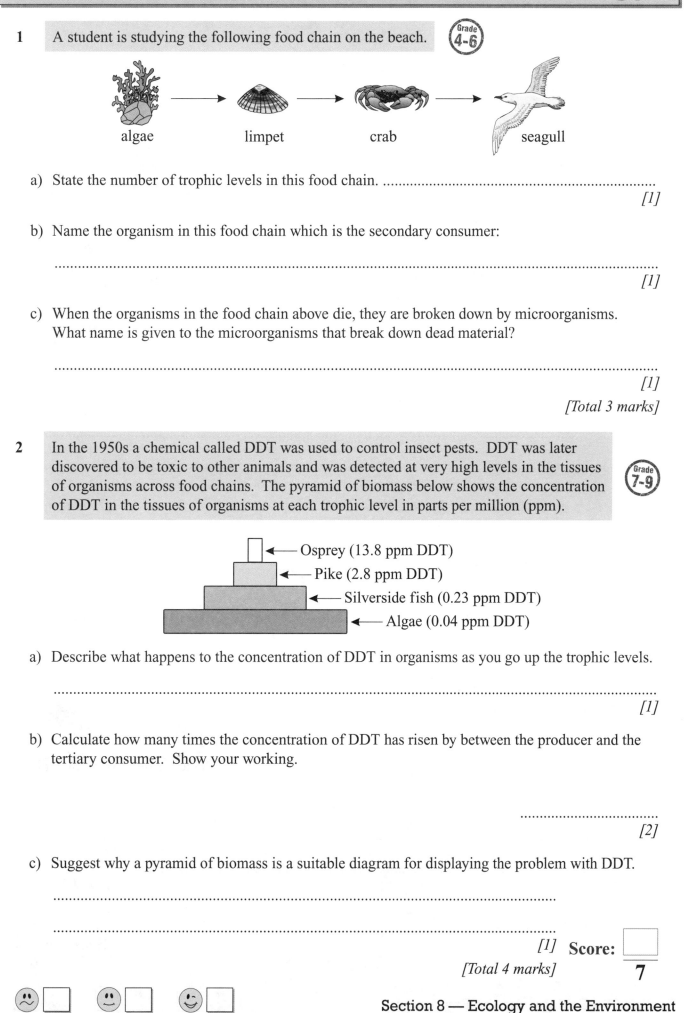

algae   limpet   crab   seagull

a) State the number of trophic levels in this food chain. ....

[1]

b) Name the organism in this food chain which is the secondary consumer:

....

[1]

c) When the organisms in the food chain above die, they are broken down by microorganisms. What name is given to the microorganisms that break down dead material?

....

[1]

[Total 3 marks]

2   In the 1950s a chemical called DDT was used to control insect pests. DDT was later discovered to be toxic to other animals and was detected at very high levels in the tissues of organisms across food chains. The pyramid of biomass below shows the concentration of DDT in the tissues of organisms at each trophic level in parts per million (ppm).   (Grade 7-9)

Osprey (13.8 ppm DDT)
Pike (2.8 ppm DDT)
Silverside fish (0.23 ppm DDT)
Algae (0.04 ppm DDT)

a) Describe what happens to the concentration of DDT in organisms as you go up the trophic levels.

....

[1]

b) Calculate how many times the concentration of DDT has risen by between the producer and the tertiary consumer. Show your working.

....

[2]

c) Suggest why a pyramid of biomass is a suitable diagram for displaying the problem with DDT.

....

....

[1]   **Score:**

[Total 4 marks]

7

Energy Transfer and Food Webs

1 A diagram of energy transfer is shown below. *(Grade 6-7)*

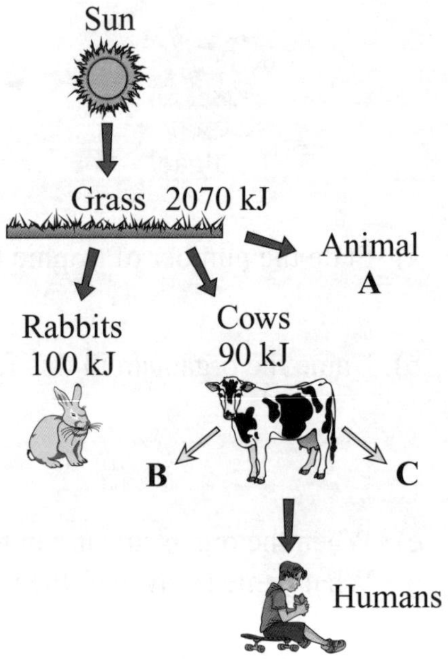

a) The efficiency of energy transfer from the grass to the next trophic level is 10%. Calculate how much energy is available to animal **A**. Show your working.

Tip: animal A is not the only organism in the second trophic level.

.... kJ
[2]

Sun

Grass 2070 kJ

Animal **A**

Rabbits 100 kJ

Cows 90 kJ

B   **C**

Humans

b) **B** and **C** are processes that represent energy loss. Suggest what these processes could be.

....

....
[2]

c) Suggest why this food chain cannot support any more trophic levels.

....

....
[2]

[Total 6 marks]

2 The diagram shows part of a food web from Nebraska, USA. The flowerhead weevil is not native to this area. It was introduced by farmers to eat the musk thistle, which is a weed. *(Grade 6-7)*

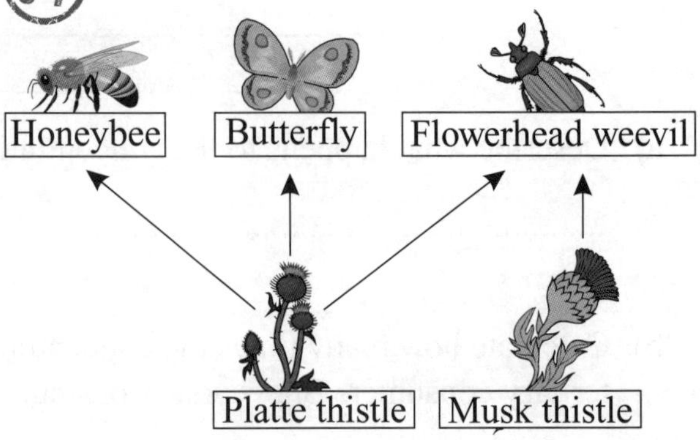

Explain how the introduction of the flowerhead weevil could affect the amount of wild honey produced in the area.

Honeybee   Butterfly   Flowerhead weevil

Platte thistle   Musk thistle

....

....

....

....

....
[Total 2 marks]

Score:

8

Section 8 — Ecology and the Environment

The Carbon Cycle

1   Carbon is constantly being recycled. The diagram on the right shows some of the processes occurring in the carbon cycle.

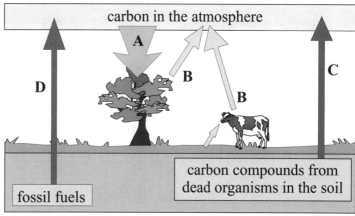

a) i) Name the process, labelled **A**, that removes carbon from the atmosphere.

....
[1]

ii) Name the gas in which carbon is removed from the atmosphere by process **A**.

....
[1]

b) Name the process, labelled **B**, by which all living organisms return carbon to the atmosphere.

....
[1]

c) Explain how carbon is released from dead organisms in the soil (process **C**).

....

....
[2]

d) i) Explain why fossil fuels contain carbon.

....

....
[1]

ii) Describe how the carbon from fossil fuels is released back into the atmosphere (process **D**).

....

....
[1]

[Total 7 marks]

Exam Practice Tip

The carbon cycle boils down to four processes: photosynthesis removes carbon dioxide from the atmosphere, while respiration, combustion and decomposition (via decomposers respiring) put it back. If you get a question on the carbon cycle, decide which of these processes are relevant before you start your answer.

Score

7

Section 8 — Ecology and the Environment

The Nitrogen Cycle

1 Several different types of bacteria are involved in the nitrogen cycle.   Grade 4-6

    a) Which bacteria convert nitrogen in the atmosphere into nitrogen compounds that plants can use?

       ☐ **A** nitrifying   ☐ **B** denitrifying   ☐ **C** nitrogen-fixing   ☐ **D** decomposers

       [1]

    b) Which bacteria break down proteins and urea into ammonia?

       ☐ **A** nitrifying   ☐ **B** denitrifying   ☐ **C** nitrogen-fixing   ☐ **D** decomposers

       [1]

    c) Which bacteria convert ammonia into nitrates?

       ☐ **A** nitrifying   ☐ **B** denitrifying   ☐ **C** nitrogen-fixing   ☐ **D** decomposers

       [1]

       [Total 3 marks]

2 Eutrophication is a process that occurs in lakes or rivers in response to the addition of excess nitrates from sources such as sewage. It results in oxygen depletion of the water, and the death of aerobic organisms such as fish. *P. denitrificans* is a species of denitrifying bacteria that can live in aerobic or anaerobic conditions.   Grade 7-9

    a) Explain why *P. denitrificans* would be a suitable organism to use to treat eutrophication in a lake.

> 'Aerobic' just means 'with oxygen' (or in the case of the fish, 'needs oxygen'). 'Anaerobic' means 'without oxygen'.

    ....

    ....

    ....

    ....

       [3]

    b) *P. denitrificans* can be found in waterlogged soils, such as those used to grow rice.
       A rice farmer wants to increase the yield of his crops by adding a nitrate-based fertiliser.
       Suggest why the presence of *P. denitrificans* in his soil may make the fertiliser less effective.

    ....

    ....

    ....

       [2]

       [Total 5 marks]

Score: ☐

8

Air Pollution

1 Carbon monoxide is an air pollutant. **(Grade 4-6)**

a) Explain how breathing in carbon monoxide reduces the amount of oxygen carried by the blood.

....

....

[1]

b) Give **one** way in which carbon monoxide is released into the atmosphere.

....

[1]

[Total 2 marks]

2 A student is investigating the local air quality. He collects data on the concentration of sulfur dioxide in the air at different sites in his town on the same day. His data is shown below. **(Grade 4-6)**

Site	Sulfur dioxide concentration (micrograms/m³)
1	9.8
2	9.4
3	7.1

a) What is the mean sulfur dioxide concentration across the three sites?

.... micrograms/m³
[2]

b) Give **one** way in which the student could have improved the reliability of his data.

....

[1]

c) Describe and explain the environmental impacts of sulfur dioxide air pollution.

....

....

....

....

....

....

[3]

[Total 6 marks]

Score: ☐

8

The Greenhouse Effect

1   Greenhouse gases are produced by many human activities.   *Grade 4-6*

Give **one** human activity that causes an increase in the atmospheric level of:

carbon dioxide,

....

methane,

....

nitrous oxides.

....

[Total 3 marks]

2   The Earth is kept warm by greenhouse gases.   *Grade 6-7*

a) Explain the role of greenhouse gases in keeping the Earth warm.

....

....

....

[2]

b) Give **one** way in which conditions on Earth would be different if there were no greenhouse gases.

....

[1]

c) Explain the relationship between greenhouse gases and global warming.

....

....

....

[3]

d) Give **one** possible consequence of global warming and explain how it could affect humans.

....

....

[2]

[Total 8 marks]

Exam Practice Tip

Don't get confused between the greenhouse effect and global warming. The greenhouse effect is a natural process that keeps the planet warm and is essential for life on Earth. Global warming is the recent increase in the mean temperature of the Earth — and the scientific consensus is that it's down to human activities.

Score

11

Section 8 — Ecology and the Environment

Water Pollution and Deforestation

1   A river flows through some farmland. Data showing the concentration
    of nitrates in the river and the average number of fish per cubic metre
    of water between 2002 and 2010 is shown below.

	2002	2004	2006	2008	2010
Nitrate concentration (mg per litre)	22	33	48	63	74
Average number of fish per m³	23	21	10	1	0

a) Describe the relationship between the nitrate concentration and the average number of fish per
    cubic metre between 2002 and 2010.

    ....
    [1]

b) Suggest an explanation for the trend in the nitrate concentration over this time period.

    ....
    [1]

c) i) Name the process illustrated by the data in the table. ....
        [1]

    ii) Explain how this process could have caused the observed change
        in the average number of fish per cubic metre of water.

        ....

        ....

        ....

        ....

        ....
        [5]

    [Total 8 marks]

2   An investigation was carried out into
    the number of microorganisms along
    a stream. A sewage outflow pipe was
    located midway along the study site.
    The results are shown to the right.

    Explain the change in number of microorganisms
    downstream from the outflow pipe.

    ....

    ....

    ....

    ....

    ....

    [Total 4 marks]

3 Read the passage below about deforestation, then answer the questions that follow. **Grade 7-9**

Forests cover around 30% of the Earth's land surface, but the
destruction of tropical forests is taking place at rapid rate.
Tropical forests are home to more than half of animal and plant species, so
this deforestation has a devastating effect on biodiversity. It is also thought
5 to contribute to global warming by disturbing the balance of carbon dioxide
in the atmosphere, as well as contributing to a drier local climate.
Studying areas that have been cleared of trees in the past provides insight into other effects of
deforestation. The Huangtu Plateau is a large area in north central China characterised by a fine,
loose soil called loess. In the past, the plateau was forested and highly fertile, but human activity
10 over the past two thousand years has greatly decreased the tree cover. The removal of trees has
been linked to increased soil erosion and increasingly infertile land. Deforestation in this area
also appears to be linked to an increasing number of natural disasters, including floods.

a) Explain how deforestation contributes to global warming (lines 5 and 6).

....

....

....

....

....

....

[4]

b) Suggest how deforestation could lead to a drier local climate (line 6).

....

....

[2]

c) Explain how the removal of trees could cause increased soil erosion (line 11).

....

....

[2]

d) Describe **one** way, other than soil erosion, in which deforestation results in infertile land (line 11).

....

....

....

....

[2]

[Total 10 marks]

Score:

22

Increasing Crop Yields

1   A farmer has three polythene tunnels which she uses to grow strawberries. She uses a different fertiliser (**A**, **B** or **C**) in each tunnel and records the strawberry yield for 5 years. Her results are shown in the table below.

a) Suggest why the farmer grows her strawberries in polythene tunnels. Explain your answer.

Fertiliser	Strawberry yield each year (kg)				
	2012	2013	2014	2015	2016
A	592	615	580	632	599
B	600	601	566	604	587
C	575	630	599	661	612

....

....

....

....

[3]

b) i) Explain which fertiliser, **A-C**, had the best effect on strawberry yield overall.

....

....

[2]

ii) Explain how fertilisers increase crop yield.

....

....

....

....

[3]

[Total 8 marks]

2   The table shows the size of the pest population and the crop yield in a farmer's field over five successive years.

a) Describe and explain the relationship between the size of the pest population and the crop yield.

Year	Estimated average pest population	Mean crop yield (tonnes)
1	10000	58
2	9000	66
3	9800	60
4	2000	88
5	2200	86

....

....

....

....

[2]

b) Suggest in which year the use of a pesticide was introduced.

....

[1]

[Total 3 marks]

Score:

11

Bacteria and Making Yoghurt

1 Yoghurt is made inside a fermenter. (Grade 3-4)

a) Which of the following microorganisms is used to produce yoghurt?

☐ **A** *Plasmodium*

☐ **B** *Lactobacillus*

☐ **C** Yeast

☐ **D** *Pneumococcus*

[1]

b) Microorganisms are used to ferment the lactose sugar that is present in milk.
The product of this reaction causes milk to clot and thicken into yoghurt.
Name the product formed in lactose fermentation that results in the production of yoghurt.

....

[1]

[Total 2 marks]

2 A fermenter is a large container used to grow microorganisms. (Grade 6-7)

a) Explain why aseptic conditions are needed inside a fermenter.

....

....

....

....

[3]

b) The diagram below shows a fermenter.

i) Explain the purpose of the air supply.

....

....

[1]

Think about the conditions microorganisms need to grow to help you answer part b).

Microorganisms in

Water out

Water-cooled jacket

Water in

Air in ↑ Product out

ii) The temperature of the fermenter is kept at an optimum level using a water-cooled jacket. Explain why the temperature needs to be prevented from getting too high inside the fermenter.

....

....

....

[1]

[Total 5 marks]

Score: ☐
7

☹ ☐   🙂 ☐   😀 ☐

Yeast and Making Bread

1   A student is investigating the effect of different factors on yeast growth. The diagram on the right shows the equipment she has set up so far. As the yeast respires, the gas produced will travel through the tube and bubble into the lime water, which will gradually turn cloudy.

(Grade 6-7)

PRACTICAL

yeast suspension

lime water

a) Name the gas produced by the respiring yeast.

....

[1]

b) Suggest **one** way in which the student could measure the respiration rate of the yeast.

....

....

[1]

c) The student wants to investigate how temperature affects the rate of respiration.

   i) Suggest how the student could alter the temperature of the yeast suspension.

....

[1]

   ii) Suggest how increasing the temperature from 20 °C to 25 °C would affect the rate of respiration.

....

[1]

[Total 4 marks]

2   A baker makes a bread dough by mixing together flour, water and yeast. *(Grade 7-9)*

The baker leaves the dough in a warm place for an hour.
Explain any changes to the bread's appearance that the baker will observe.

....

....

....

....

....

....

[Total 5 marks]

Exam Practice Tip

Make sure you know the difference between 'describe' and 'explain'. You'll miss out on marks if you just describe a process or observation instead of explaining <u>why</u> it happens. And make sure that you don't waste time explaining something when you only need to describe it — it won't gain you any extra marks.

Score

9

Selective Breeding

1 The characteristics of two varieties of wheat plants are shown in the table below.

Variety	Grain yield	Resistance to bad weather
Tall stems	High	Low
Dwarf stems	Low	High

Describe how selective breeding could be used to create a wheat plant
with a high grain yield and high resistance to bad weather.

....

....

....

....

[Total 3 marks]

2 The graph below shows the milk yield for a population of cows over three generations.

Key: Generation 1 ——
Generation 2 ——
Generation 3 ------

a) Do you think that selective breeding is likely to have been used with these cows?
Explain your answer.

....

....

[1]

b) Calculate the increase in the average milk yield per year per cow
between generation 1 and generation 3.

.... litres per year per cow

[2]

[Total 3 marks]

Score:

6

Fish Farming

1 Fish farms are controlled environments designed to produce many fish. (Grade 4-6)

   a) i) Suggest what must be removed from the water in fish farms to maintain the water quality.

....

[1]

       ii) Name **one** other factor that needs to be monitored to make sure the water quality is maintained.

....

[1]

   b) Suggest why the fish tanks in fish farms are covered over.

....

[1]

   c) i) Explain what is meant by the term intraspecific predation.

....

[1]

       ii) Give **one** way in which intraspecific predation can be avoided on a fish farm.

....

[1]

   d) Suggest how it may be possible for fish with more
       desirable characteristics to be produced at a fish farm.

....

[1]

[Total 6 marks]

2 Fish can be farmed in cages in the sea or in indoor tanks. Describe an investigation to find out which of these methods results in the highest growth rate of fish. (Grade 7-9)

....

....

....

....

....

....

[Total 6 marks]

Exam Practice Tip

If you're asked to describe an investigation, start with the basics of the method, e.g. you'd take some organisms, divide them into two groups, treat one group one way and treat the other group a different way. Then include details on what you'd measure, how and when, and what things you'd keep the same in both groups.

Score

[ ]

12

 [ ]   [ ]   [ ]

Section 9 — Use of Biological Resources

Genetic Engineering

1 The image on the right shows a tomato grown on a transgenic plant.

Grade 4-6

State the main way in which the genes of the tomato shown will differ from those found in a tomato grown on a non-transgenic plant.

....

....

[Total 1 mark]

2 Genetic engineering can be used to produce large amounts of human insulin.

Grade 4-6

The statements below describe the first two steps involved in the genetic engineering of human insulin.

1. The human insulin gene is cut from human DNA.

2. A plasmid from a bacterial cell is cut open.

a) Which row of the table correctly shows the enzymes involved in the two steps described above?

		Step 1	Step 2
☐	**A**	restriction	restriction
☐	**B**	ligase	ligase
☐	**C**	restriction	ligase
☐	**D**	ligase	restriction

[1]

b) State the vector involved in the production of human insulin.

....

[1]

c) The next step in the production of human insulin is to produce recombinant DNA. Describe what is meant by the term **recombinant DNA**.

....

[1]

d) Describe how large amounts of human insulin are made from the recombinant DNA.

....

....

....

....

[3]

[Total 6 marks]

3 Read the article below about GM crops and answer the questions that follow.

Recently some farmers took part in crop trials to see what effects growing herbicide-resistant GM crops might have on wildlife. They used four kinds of crops in the trials. In each case, the farmer split one of their normal fields in half. They then grew a 'normal' crop in one half and its
5 GM equivalent in the other. With the GM crops, the farmers followed instructions about how much of which herbicides to use, and when to apply them. They applied herbicides to the 'normal' crop as they usually would. As the crops grew, the researchers monitored the populations of insects, slugs, spiders and other wildlife in each environment.

10 The researchers found that with three kinds of crops, growing normal crops was better for wildlife — they found more butterflies and bees on the normal crops. With the fourth crop, the opposite seemed to be true — there were slightly more butterflies and bees around the GM crops.

a) i) Suggest why each field was divided in half rather than choosing separate fields for normal and GM crops (lines 3 and 4).

....

....

[2]

ii) Suggest **one** thing the researchers may have done to improve the reliability of the trial.

....

[1]

b) Some people are worried that growing GM crops will reduce the variety of wildlife in the environment. Do you think the results of the trial support this concern? Explain your answer.

....

....

[1]

c) Other than the effect on the variety of wildlife, give **two** reasons why people may be concerned about the production of GM crops.

1 ....

2 ....

[2]

d) Crops can also be genetically modified to be pest-resistant. Suggest how growing pest-resistant crops in the UK could benefit farmers.

....

....

[1]

[Total 7 marks]

Score:

14

Section 9 — Use of Biological Resources

Cloning

1 Some animals can be genetically engineered to produce useful human proteins in their milk.

Grade 4-6

a) Give **one** reason why these animals would then be cloned, rather than being left to reproduce naturally.

....

....

[1]

b) Suggest **one** possible risk involved with cloning animals.

....

....

[1]

[Total 2 marks]

2 Dolly the sheep was cloned by transplanting a cell nucleus.

Grade 6-7

a) Which of the following describes the process used to clone Dolly?

☐ **A** A haploid nucleus from a sheep egg cell was inserted into an enucleated mature udder cell of the same sheep.

☐ **B** A diploid nucleus from a mature sheep udder cell was inserted into an enucleated egg cell of the same sheep.

☐ **C** A haploid nucleus from a sheep egg cell was inserted into an enucleated mature udder cell of a different sheep.

☐ **D** A diploid nucleus from a mature sheep udder cell was inserted into an enucleated egg cell of a different sheep.

[1]

b) i) Plants can also be cloned. Describe how plants are cloned using micropropagation.

....

....

....

....

[4]

ii) Explain why micropropagation is beneficial for commercial farmers.

....

[1]

[Total 6 marks]

Score: ☐

8

Candidate Surname		Candidate Forename(s)	

Centre Number	Candidate Number

Edexcel International GCSE

Biology
Paper 1B

Practice Paper
Time allowed: 2 hours

You must have:	Total marks:
• A ruler.	
• A calculator.	

Instructions to candidates

* Use **black** ink to write your answers.
* Write your name and other details in the spaces provided above.
* Answer **all** questions in the spaces provided.
* In calculations, show clearly how you worked out your answers.
* You will need to answer some questions by placing a cross in a box, like this: ☒
  To change your answer, draw a line through the box like this: ☒
  Then mark your new answer as normal.

Information for candidates

* The marks available are given in brackets at the end of each question.
* There are 110 marks available for this paper.

Advice for candidates

* Read all the questions carefully.
* Write your answers as clearly and neatly as possible.
* Keep in mind how much time you have left.

Answer **all** questions

1   The diagram below shows the human male and female reproductive systems.

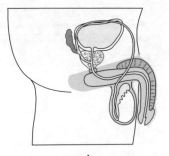 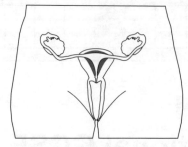

male
reproductive system   female
reproductive system

(a)   Cells in the reproductive systems undergo cell division to produce gametes.
       Gametes contain half the usual number of chromosomes.

   (i)   Give the word that describes cells that contain half the usual number of chromosomes.

   ....
                                                                                                                                   [1]

   (ii)   In humans, how many chromosomes does one gamete contain?

          ☐ **A** 12

          ☐ **B** 23

          ☐ **C** 32

          ☐ **D** 46

                                                                                                                                   [1]

   (iii) Which of the following structures in the human male reproductive system is the site of
          gamete production?

          ☐ **A** vas deferens

          ☐ **B** testes

          ☐ **C** urethra

          ☐ **D** erectile tissue

                                                                                                                                   [1]

(b)   An embryo develops in the female reproductive system.
       Describe how a human embryo is formed.

   ....

   ....

   ....
                                                                                                                                   [3]
                                                                                                                   [Total 6 marks]

2   Some pondweed was used to investigate how the amount of light available affects the rate of photosynthesis.

The apparatus that was used for this experiment is shown below.

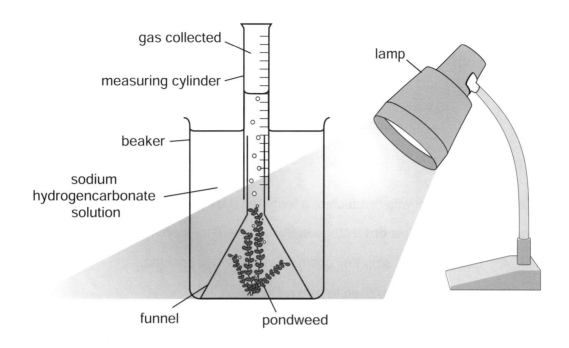

(a)   Name the gas that is being collected in the measuring cylinder.

....

[1]

(b)   Explain what would happen to the volume of gas collected if the investigation was repeated with the lamp turned off.

....

....

....

[3]

(c)   Sodium hydrogencarbonate dissolves in water and releases carbon dioxide.
Suggest why sodium hydrogencarbonate was added to the water in this experiment.

....

....

....

[2]

Turn over ▶

Practice Paper 1B

(d) Explain how temperature affects the rate of photosynthesis, and suggest how temperature could be controlled in the experiment.

....

....

....

....

....

....

[3]

After the experiment was conducted, a leaf from the pondweed was tested for starch.

(e) (i) Which of the following is **not** a stage in testing a leaf for starch?

☐ **A** Boil the leaf to stop any chemical reactions happening.

☐ **B** Dry the leaf in an oven to remove water.

☐ **C** Heat the leaf with ethanol to remove chlorophyll.

☐ **D** Add a few drops of iodine solution.

[1]

(ii) Would you expect the test to produce a positive result? Explain your answer.

....

....

[1]

[Total 11 marks]

3   The diagram below shows nutrients being absorbed from the gut into the blood.

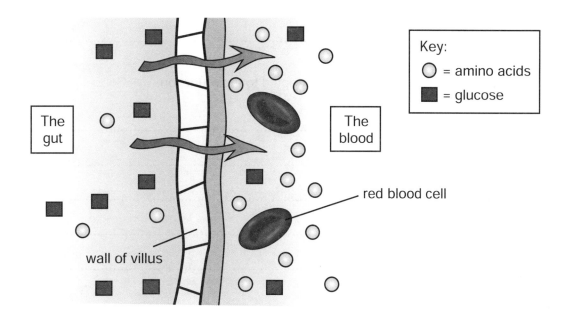

(a)   Describe **three** ways that villi are adapted to absorb the products of digestion.

....

....

....

....

....

[3]

(b)   The diagram shows glucose being absorbed into the blood by diffusion.
       Describe how the amino acids are absorbed into the blood.

....

....

....

[2]

(c)   The diagram shows red blood cells in the blood.

(i)   State the function of red blood cells.

....

[1]

(ii) Explain how red blood cells are adapted to their function.

....

....

....

....

....

[3]

[Total 9 marks]

4 A student grew three plants in a windowsill tray. This is shown in Diagram 1.

He then put the plants in a cardboard box with a cut-out hole. This is shown in Diagram 2.

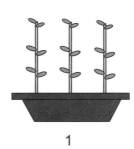

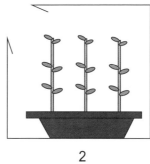

1   2

(a) (i) Draw a diagram to show how you would expect the plants in the box to look after 3 days.

[1]

(ii) Explain what caused the plants' response.

....

....

....

....

....

....

[4]

(b) Which of the following responses is shown by the plants in this experiment?

☐ **A** positive phototropism

☐ **B** negative phototropism

☐ **C** positive geotropism

☐ **D** negative geotropism

[1]

[Total 6 marks]

Turn over ▶

Practice Paper 1B

5   Cystic fibrosis is a genetic disorder caused by a recessive allele.

A couple have a baby boy. The doctor tells them that the baby has inherited cystic fibrosis.
Neither parent shows signs of the disorder.

(a) (i)   In the space below, construct a diagram to show how the baby inherited cystic fibrosis.

Your diagram should show the genotypes of both parents, the genotypes of their gametes,
and all the possible genotypes of their offspring.

Use **F** to represent the dominant allele and **f** to represent the recessive allele.

[3]

(ii) Is the baby homozygous or heterozygous for this condition?
Explain your answer.

....

....
[1]

(b)   The doctor tells the parents that if they have another child,
the fetus can be tested to see if it will have cystic fibrosis.

State the probability that the couple's next baby will have cystic fibrosis.

....
[1]

The family pedigree below shows a family with a history of cystic fibrosis.

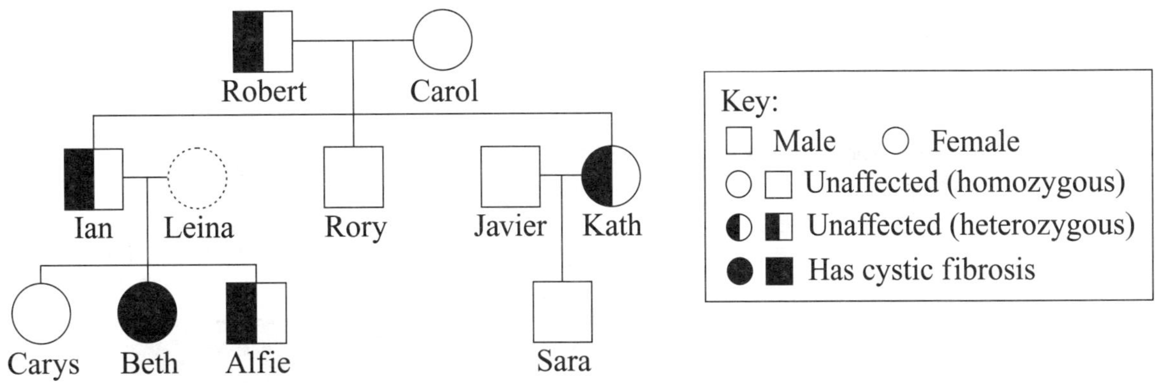

Robert
Carol
Ian
Leina
Rory
Javier
Kath
Carys
Beth
Alfie
Sara
Key:
Male
Female
Unaffected (homozygous)
Unaffected (heterozygous)
Has cystic fibrosis

(c) Using the information given above, explain what Leina's genotype must be.

....

....

....

[2]

(d) Carys and Beth are sisters. Carys has a scar on her hand. Beth does not.

Explain whether this is an example of genetic variation, environmental variation, or a combination of both.

....

....

....

[2]

[Total 9 marks]

Turn over ▶

6   The peppered moth is an insect that lives on the trunks of trees in Britain.
The moths are prey for birds such as thrushes.

The peppered moth exists in two varieties:

1. A light-coloured variety — they are
better camouflaged on tree trunks in
unpolluted areas.

2. A dark-coloured variety — they are
better camouflaged on sooty
tree trunks in badly polluted areas.

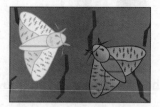

The dark variety of the moth was first recorded in the north of England in 1848.
It became increasingly common in polluted areas until the 1960s, when the number
of soot-covered trees declined because of the introduction of new laws.

(a)   Using the idea of natural selection, explain why the dark variety of moth became more
common in soot-polluted areas.

....

....

....

....

....

[4]

The following bar charts show the percentages of dark- and light-coloured peppered moths in two different towns.

Town **A**

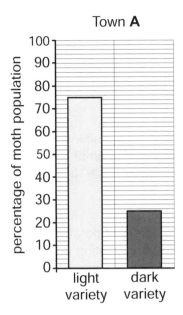

Town **B**

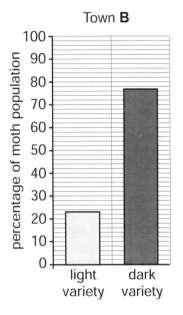

(b)   State which town, **A** or **B**, is the most polluted. Give a reason for your answer.

....

....

[1]

(c)   Calculate the difference in percentage between the dark-coloured moth population in Town **A** and Town **B**. Show your working.

...........................%

[2]

[Total 7 marks]

Turn over ▶

Practice Paper 1B

A student carried out an experiment to investigate osmosis.

The student cut cylinders out of potatoes and placed them into different concentrations of sugar solution, as shown in the diagram below.

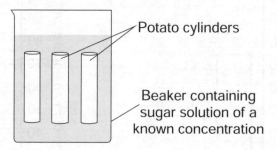

Potato cylinders

Beaker containing
sugar solution of a
known concentration

The student then measured the mass of the cylinders of potato before and after they had been placed in different concentrations of sugar solution for 20 minutes.
The student's results are shown below.

Concentration of sugar solution (M)	Change in mass (g)			Mean change in mass (g)
	Potato cylinder 1	Potato cylinder 2	Potato cylinder 3	
0.0	+0.67	+0.65	+0.69	+0.67
0.2	+0.30	+0.31	+0.33	+0.31
0.4	+0.02	−0.02	+0.01	0
0.6	−0.27	−0.31	−0.25	−0.28
0.8	−0.48	−0.50	−0.47	−0.48
1.0	−0.71	−0.65	−0.72	−0.69
1.2	−0.78	−0.81	−0.82	

(a)   Calculate the mean change in mass in a 1.2 M sugar solution.
Show your working.

.... g

[2]

(b)   Draw a graph of the concentration of sugar solution against the mean change in mass on the grid below.   Use straight lines to join the points.

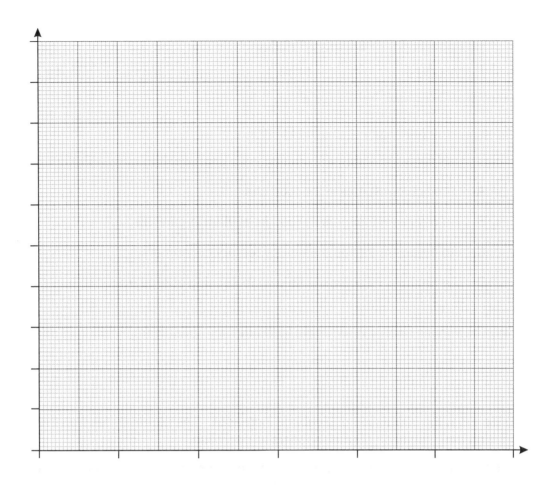

[6]

(c)   Estimate the concentration of sugar inside the original potatoes.
Explain your answer.

....

....

....

[2]

(d)   Suggest why the student used three potato cylinders in each concentration of sugar solution, and took a mean of the results.

....

[1]

[Total 11 marks]

8 The diagram below shows the amount of energy contained within an area of plants. It shows how much energy from the plants is transferred to each trophic level in a food chain.

plants	→	grasshoppers	→	mice	→	snakes
11 000 J		1100 J		130 J		12 J

(a) (i) Plants are the producers in this food chain.

Which of the following statements describes a producer?

☐ **A** The first consumer in the food chain.

☐ **B** An organism that gets its food from other organisms.

☐ **C** An organism that gets eaten by tertiary consumers.

☐ **D** An organism that makes its own food using energy from the Sun.

[1]

(ii) State how much energy is available to the tertiary consumers in this food chain.

....

[1]

(iii) In the area, the population of bluebirds increases. The bluebirds feed on the grasshoppers, causing the population of grasshoppers to decrease.

Suggest **one** way that the change in grasshopper population may affect the population of another organism in this food chain. Explain your answer.

....

....

[2]

Four pyramids of biomass are shown below.

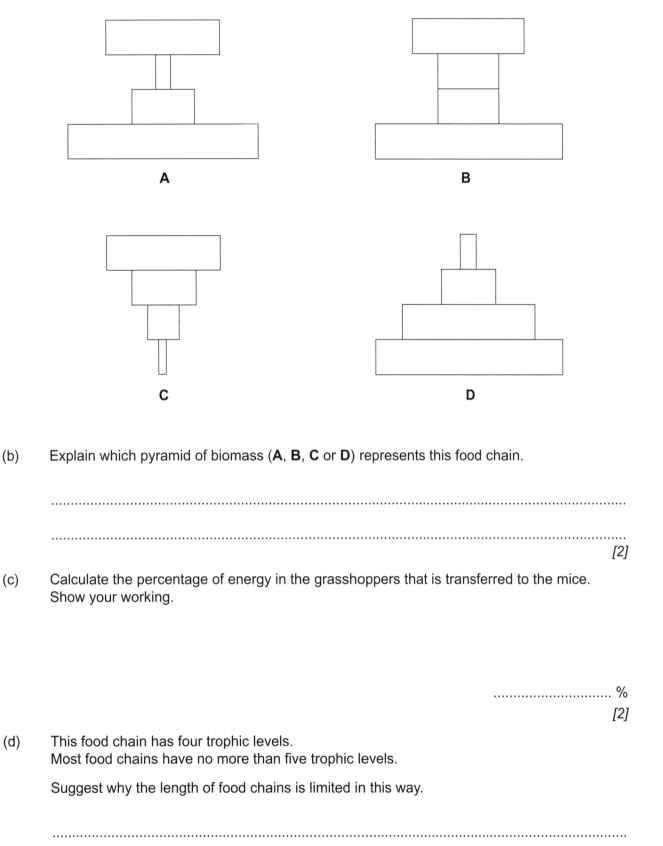

A B C D

(b) Explain which pyramid of biomass (**A**, **B**, **C** or **D**) represents this food chain.

....

....

[2]

(c) Calculate the percentage of energy in the grasshoppers that is transferred to the mice.
Show your working.

.... %

[2]

(d) This food chain has four trophic levels.
Most food chains have no more than five trophic levels.

Suggest why the length of food chains is limited in this way.

....

....

....

[2]

[Total 10 marks]

Turn over ▶

Practice Paper 1B

9   The diagram below shows an alveolus and a blood capillary.

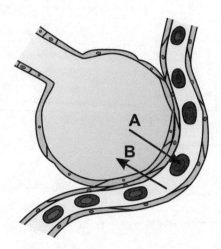

(a)   The arrows on the diagram show the net movement of two gases, **A** and **B**.

Name gases **A** and **B**.

Gas **A** ....

Gas **B** ....

[2]

(b)   Explain **three** ways that alveoli are adapted for gas exchange.

....

....

....

....

[3]

(c)   Ventilation allows air to enter and leave the lungs.

Describe the process that results in air leaving the lungs.

....

....

....

[4]

[Total 9 marks]

10 Describe an investigation to find out if lettuces grown in a polythene tunnel have a faster growth rate than those grown outside.

....

....

....

....

....

....

....

....

....

....

....

....

[Total 6 marks]

Turn over ▶

11 Two students carried out an experiment to investigate the effects of different minerals on plant growth. Their teacher gave them three pea plants of the same species, all of a similar height. The method they used is described below.

> **1.** Measure the height of the three pea plants.
>
> **2.** Add a solution containing minerals to three beakers as follows:
>
> > Beaker A: solution high in magnesium and nitrates.
> >
> > Beaker B: solution high in magnesium and low in nitrates.
> >
> > Beaker C: solution low in magnesium and high in nitrates.
>
> **3.** Place a pea plant in each of the beakers, A, B and C.
>
> **4.** Leave the plants to grow for one week.
>
> **5.** Measure the height of each of the plants at the end of the week.

The results of the experiment are shown below.

Beaker	Height at start (cm)	Height at end (cm)	Change in height (cm)
A	4	9	5
B	5	7	2
C	4	8	4

(a) Explain why the growth in beaker B was poor.

....

....

....

[3]

(b) Describe how you would expect the pea plant in beaker C, which was low in magnesium, to look at the end of the week. Explain your answer.

....

....

[2]

(c) State **two** factors that the students would have had to keep the same in each beaker to make the experiment a fair test.

1 ....

2 ....

[2]

[Total 7 marks]

12   A study collected data from a sample of male British doctors.
      It compared the death rate from coronary heart disease per 1000 men
      per year to the number of cigarettes smoked each day.

      The results are shown in the graph below.

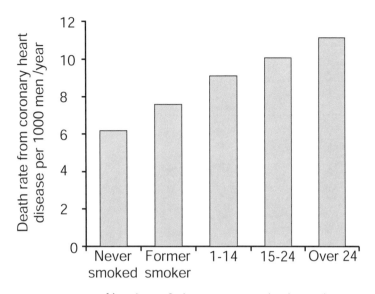

(a) (i)   What conclusions can you draw from this graph?

      ....

      ....

      ....

      ....

      ....

                                                                                                                          [3]

   (ii) A scientist hypothesises that anyone who smokes is more likely to die from
         coronary heart disease.

         Suggest **one** change you could make to the study above to test this hypothesis.

      ....

      ....

                                                                                                                          [1]

112

(b)   Describe and explain **two** effects of smoking on the lungs.

1 ....

....

....

2 ....

....

....

[4]

[Total 8 marks]

13 A student is investigating how his heart rate changes during and after exercise. He measures his heart rate using a portable heart rate monitor. He takes his resting heart rate then immediately runs around a running track for two minutes. Then he rests again. His results are shown on the graph below.

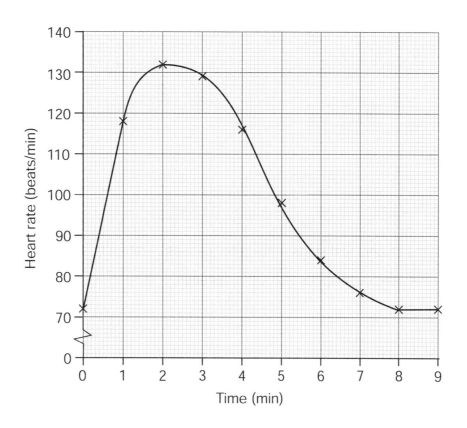

(a) Give the independent variable in the student's experiment.

....

[1]

(b) Use the graph to estimate the student's heart rate after 90 seconds.

....

[1]

(c) The student stopped running two minutes after taking his first heart rate measurement. How long did it take for his heart rate to return to normal after he stopped running?

....

[1]

Turn over ▶

(d)   Explain how the student's heart rate changes with exercise.

....

....

....

....

....

....

....

....

[5]

(e)   When ths student first starts running he respires aerobically.

(i)   Write the word equation for aerobic respiration.

....

[2]

(ii)   Give **one** advantage of aerobic respiration over anaerobic respiration.

....

....

[1]

[Total 11 marks]

[Total for paper 110 marks]

Candidate Surname	Candidate Forename(s)

Centre Number	Candidate Number

Edexcel
International GCSE

Biology
Paper 2B

Practice Paper
Time allowed: 1 hour 15 minutes

You must have:
- A ruler.
- A calculator.

Total marks:

Instructions to candidates
- Use **black** ink to write your answers.
- Write your name and other details in the spaces provided above.
- Answer **all** questions in the spaces provided.
- In calculations, show clearly how you worked out your answers.
- You will need to answer some questions by placing a cross in a box, like this: ☒
  To change your answer, draw a line through the box like this: ☒
  Then mark your new answer as normal.

Information for candidates
- The marks available are given in brackets at the end of each question.
- There are 70 marks available for this paper.

Advice for candidates
- Read all the questions carefully.
- Write your answers as clearly and neatly as possible.
- Keep in mind how much time you have left.

Answer **all** questions

1   Read the passage below, then answer the questions that follow.

Genetically modified crops — Golden Rice

Vitamin A deficiency is a major health problem across the world — particularly in developing countries in South Asia and parts of Africa. A lack of dietary vitamin A makes people more vulnerable to disease and more likely to die from infections. It's also a primary cause of preventable blindness in children, and can contribute to women dying during
5   pregnancy or shortly after childbirth.

To try to address this problem, scientists from across the world have worked together to develop a type of transgenic rice, named Golden Rice. The rice has been genetically engineered to contain a gene from a maize plant and a gene from a soil bacterium, which together allow the rice to synthesise a compound known as beta-carotene.

10   Beta-carotene is an orange pigment which occurs naturally in a range of different plants and fruits. It is also known as provitamin A. In the body it is an early component of the chemical pathway that leads to the production of vitamin A, so a larger amount of beta-carotene in the diet allows the production of a larger amount of vitamin A.

Rice is widely eaten in many areas where vitamin A deficiency is a problem. However,
15   normal rice does not contain any beta-carotene and is therefore not a source of vitamin A. In contrast, it is estimated that an adult would only need to eat around 150 g (uncooked) of Golden Rice per day in order to obtain the estimated average daily requirement (EAR) of vitamin A.

Eating a small amount of Golden Rice is a simple solution to the problem of insufficient
20   dietary vitamin A. Farmers in the developing world can grow their own Golden Rice and protect themselves and others from the negative health impacts of vitamin A deficiency, without having to rely on dietary supplements such as vitamin tablets.

(a) Unlike in many developing countries (lines 1-2), vitamin A deficiency is not a major health problem in developed countries such as the UK.

Suggest **one** reason why this is the case.

....

....

[1]

(b) (i) Apart from Golden Rice, name a food that is a good source of vitamin A.

....

[1]

(ii) Which of the following is a function of vitamin A in the human body?

☐ **A** making haemoglobin

☐ **B** providing energy

☐ **C** maintaining a healthy visual system

☐ **D** aiding the movement of food through the gut

[1]

(c) Golden Rice is a **transgenic organism** (line 7).
Explain what this means with reference to the passage.

....

....

....

[1]

(d) Suggest why beta-carotene is also known as provitamin A (line 11).

....

....

[1]

(e) Golden Rice has been genetically modified to increase its nutrient content (line 9).
Describe **two** other ways in which organisms can be genetically modified to benefit humans.

1 ....

....

2 ....

....

[2]

Turn over ▶

(f)   There are different ways of estimating how much vitamin A a person needs in their diet.
EAR is one. Recommended daily allowance (RDA) is another.

The EAR for vitamin A (lines 16-17) is around 70% of the RDA.

Calculate how much Golden Rice an adult would need to eat to obtain 100% of the
RDA of vitamin A. Show your working.

.... g

[2]

(g)   Suggest and explain why farmers who grow Golden Rice to supply their dietary vitamin A
may be financially better off than if they regularly bought vitamin A tablets.

....

....

....

[2]

(h)   With some genetically modified crop plants, farmers are not allowed to save seeds at the
end of a growing season and replant them the following year. The project behind Golden
Rice does allow farmers in the developing world to save seed from Golden Rice plants.

Suggest why this is beneficial to farmers in the developing world.

....

....

....

[2]

[Total 13 marks]

2   The diagram below shows the nitrogen cycle.
    The labels **A-D** represent different stages of the cycle.

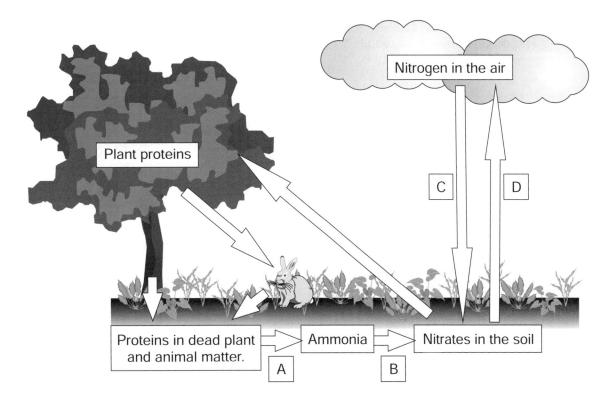

(a)   Complete the table by writing in the types of bacteria that are involved
      at each of the stages **A-D**. The first one has been done for you.

Stage	Type of Bacteria
A	Decomposers
B	
C	
D	

[3]

(b)   Decomposers also play a role in the carbon cycle.
      Explain the role of decomposers in the carbon cycle.

....

....

....

[2]

[Total 5 marks]

Turn over ▶

3   Environmental officers studied a river that was polluted by sewage.

They measured the amount of dissolved oxygen in the river at different points along its length. The flow of water is from point 1 towards point 15.

The graph shows their results.

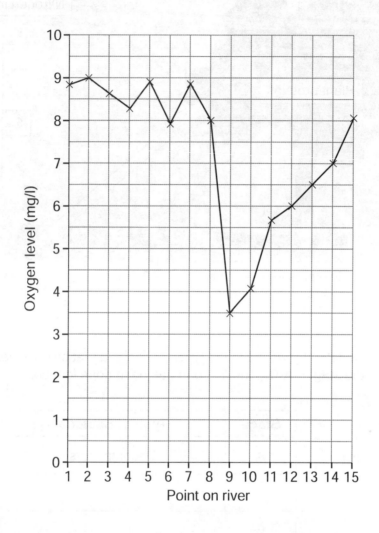

(a)   Using the information in the graph, state where the source of pollution is located. Give a reason for your answer.

....

....

[2]

(b)   The larvae of an insect known as a mayfly can be used to estimate pollution levels in water. Mayfly larvae cannot survive in polluted water.

Suggest how the population size of mayfly larvae at **point 1** would differ from the population size at **point 10**.

....

....

[1]

(c)   Explain how the pollution of water by sewage affects the oxygen level in the water.

....

....

....

....

....

....

....
                                                                                                          [4]

(d)   A survey was carried out into the number of birds feeding along the river.

Although fairly common elsewhere, few herons were spotted feeding near the source of the pollution.

Suggest an explanation for this.

....

....

....
                                                                                                          [2]

(e)   Calculate the range of the dissolved oxygen concentration measured along the length of the river.

.... mg/l
                                                                                                          [1]
                                                                                                    [10 marks]

Turn over ▶

Practice Paper 2B

4   An experiment was carried out to discover the best growth medium for the tissue culture of a certain species of plant. Four different growth media, 1 - 4, were used.

The scientists weighed ten blocks of stem tissue, each measuring 1 mm × 1 mm × 1 mm. These were placed onto growth medium 1, as shown in the diagram.

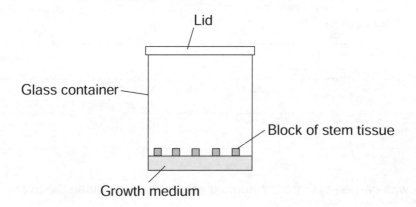

The container was then incubated at 35 °C for two days. At the end of that time, the blocks were taken out and weighed again to see how much they had grown.

This was repeated with the other three growth media.

The whole experiment was repeated again, using root tissue instead of stem tissue.

The results of the experiments are shown in the table.

| | Average % increase in mass | |
Growth medium	Stem tissue	Root tissue
1	120	77
2	85	62
3	65	58
4	98	102

(a)   Draw a bar chart to represent the average percentage increase in mass for stem and root tissue in each growth medium.

[5]

(b)   Which combination of plant tissue and growth medium produced the best results? Explain your answer.

....

....

[2]

(c)   Give **two** variables that needed to be controlled in this experiment.

1 ....

2 ....

[2]

(d)   Which of the following is another name for tissue culture?

☐ **A**   selective breeding

☐ **B**   genetic engineering

☐ **C**   differentiation

☐ **D**   micropropagation

[1]

(e)   Tissue culture is an example of asexual reproduction.

Give **three** differences between asexual and sexual reproduction.

1 ....

....

....

2 ....

....

....

3 ....

....

....

[3]
[Total 13 marks]

5   The menstrual cycle is controlled by the hormones FSH, oestrogen, LH and progesterone.

(a)   Name the part of the body where the hormone FSH is produced.

....
                                                                                                                                    [1]

(b)   Describe the roles of the hormones involved in the menstrual cycle.

....

....

....

....

....

....

....

....

....

....
                                                                                                                                    [6]
                                                                                                                          [Total 7 marks]

Turn over ▶

6 The diagram below shows the structure of a DNA double-stranded helix. The two strands are held together by cross-linking between their bases.

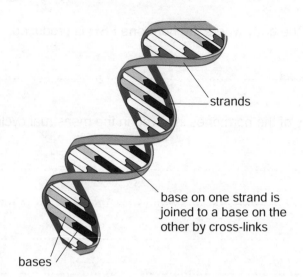

strands

base on one strand is joined to a base on the other by cross-links

bases

(a) Explain why there will always be equal amounts of bases A and T in a molecule of DNA.

....

....

[1]

(b) Name the part of a cell where strands of human DNA are found.

....

[1]

A sequence of bases in a section of DNA is shown below.

A T C A G G C T A G T T

(c) State the number of amino acids that the base sequence would code for.

....

[1]

A mutation occurs in the base sequence of the section of DNA.
The mutation is shown in the diagram below.

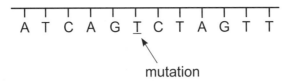

mutation

The mutation does not result in a change of phenotype.

(d) (i)   Which of the following describes the term phenotype?

☐   **A**   The combination of alleles that an individual has.

☐   **B**   Having two alleles that are the same.

☐   **C**   The characteristics produced by alleles.

☐   **D**   Having two different dominant alleles.

[1]

(ii)   Suggest **two** reasons why the mutation does not have an affect on phenotype.

....

....

....

....

[2]

[Total 6 marks]

Turn over ▶

Practice Paper 2B

7   A student did an experiment to investigate the effect of pH on the action of the enzyme amylase. The method used is shown below.

---

1. Add a set quantity of starch solution to a test tube and the same quantity of amylase solution to another.
2. Add a set quantity of a buffer solution with a pH of 5 to the tube containing starch solution.
3. Place the test tubes in a water bath at 35 °C.
4. Allow the starch and amylase solutions to reach the temperature of the water bath, then mix them together and return the mixture to the water bath.
5. Take a small sample of the mixture every minute and test for starch.
6. Stop the experiment when starch is no longer present in the sample, or after 30 minutes (whichever is sooner).
7. Repeat the experiment using buffer solutions of different pH values.

(a)   Describe what happens to the starch solution during the experiment.

....

[1]

(b)   Explain why a set quantity of starch solution was used for each repeat in the experiment.

....

....

[1]

The graph below shows the student's results.

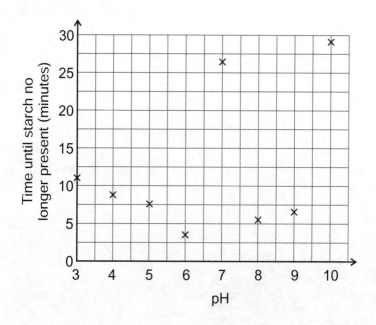

(c)   Explain the results between **pH 9** and **pH 10**.

....▶

....

....

....

....

[3]

(d) (i)   The student thinks that one of the results shown on the graph is likely to be anomalous.
Identify the anomalous result and give a reason for your answer.

....

....

[2]

(ii)   Suggest what the student might have done to cause this anomalous result.

....

....

[1]
[Total 8 marks]

8   The kidneys play a crucial role in filtering the blood.
The diagram shows a kidney nephron and the blood vessels associated with it.

(a)   Label the glomerulus and the loop of Henle on the diagram.

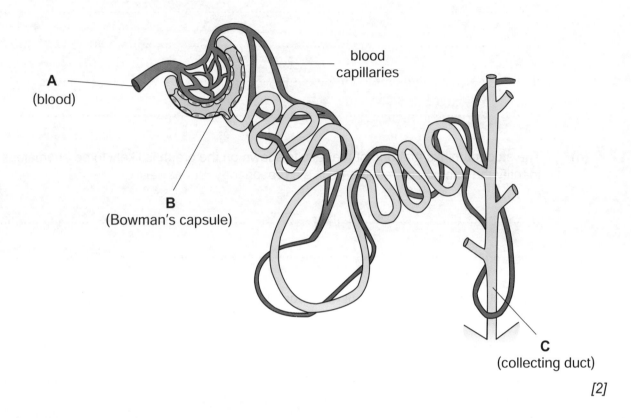

[2]

(b)   Many different proteins are found in the blood at point **A** on the diagram,
but hardly any are found at point **B**.

Explain why there is almost no protein at point **B**.

....

....

[1]

(c) (i)   The concentration of urea is greatest at point **C**. Explain why.

....

....

[1]

(ii) Explain how the concentration of sugar at point **C** would compare to the concentration at point **B**.

....

....

....

[2]

(d)   Describe the effect of ADH on the kidney nephron.

....

....

[2]

[Total 8 marks]

[Total for paper 70 marks]

Answers

Section 1 — The Nature and Variety of Organisms

Page 3 — Characteristics of Living Organisms

1 a) Any three from: e.g. they feed, which means they require nutrition. / They are sensitive to chemicals in the water, allowing them to detect food. This shows they can respond to changes in their environment. / They are able to travel towards food, showing that they can move. / They release eggs/sperm, which suggests they reproduce. *[3 marks]*

b) To obtain nutrients / for nutrition *[1 mark]*.

c) respiration *[1 mark]*

d) Excretion is the process of removing waste products *[1 mark]*.

e) E.g. it may be smaller. / It may not be fully developed. *[1 mark]*

f) It shows they are able to control their internal conditions *[1 mark]*.

Page 4 — Levels of Organisation

1 a) It is an organelle surrounded by its own membrane *[1 mark]*. It contains genetic material *[1 mark]*.

b) i) Chloroplasts are the site of photosynthesis *[1 mark]*.

ii) The vacuole helps to support the cell *[1 mark]*.

c) Tissues, organs, organ systems *[2 marks for correct answers in correct order, otherwise 1 mark for correct answers]*.

2 a) i) X — cell membrane *[1 mark]*
Y — cytoplasm *[1 mark]*

ii) E.g.

cellulose

[1 mark for an arrow pointing to anywhere on the cell wall]

b) Similarities — any two from: e.g. both an animal cell and a plant cell have a cell membrane. / Both an animal cell and a plant cell have a nucleus. / Both an animal cell and a plant cell have cytoplasm. / Both an animal cell and a plant cell have mitochondria. / Both an animal cell and a plant cell have ribosomes *[2 marks]*.
Differences — any two from: e.g. an animal cell doesn't have a vacuole, but a plant cell does. / An animal cell doesn't have a cell wall, but a plant cell does. / An animal cell doesn't contain chloroplasts, but a plant cell does. *[2 marks]*

Page 5 — Specialised Cells and Stem Cells

1 C *[1 mark]*

2 a) They have the potential to turn into any different cell type *[1 mark]*, so they could be used to replace the damaged cells in the spinal cord *[1 mark]*.

b) E.g. the stem cells are grown in the lab and may become contaminated with a virus *[1 mark]* which could be passed on to the patient and so make them sicker *[1 mark]*.

c) E.g. some people believe that human embryos shouldn't be used because each one is a potential human life *[1 mark]*.

d) Adult stem cells cannot turn/differentiate into any type of human cell, only certain ones *[1 mark]*.

Page 6 — Plants, Animals and Fungi

1 B *[1 mark]*

2 a) It is made up of thread-like structures called hyphae *[1 mark]*, which contain lots of nuclei *[1 mark]*.

b) B *[1 mark]*

3 a) Organism A is an insect because animal cells don't have a cell wall *[1 mark]*.

b) saprotrophic nutrition *[1 mark]*

c) Insect because it is an animal, and so has nervous coordination *[1 mark]*.

Page 7 — Protoctists, Bacteria and Viruses

1 a) C *[1 mark]*

b) E.g. *Amoeba* *[1 mark]*

2 a) i) A, because *Lactobacillus bulgaricus* is rod-shaped *[1 mark]*. Pneumococcus *bacteria are spherical (like the bacteria in diagram B).*

ii) It can be used to produce yoghurt from milk *[1 mark]*.

b) A pathogen is an organism that can cause disease *[1 mark]*.

c) Any three from: e.g. it has a cell wall. / It has a cell membrane. / It has cytoplasm. / It has plasmids. / It has a circular chromosome of DNA. / It doesn't have a nucleus. *[3 marks]*

3 a) The tobacco mosaic virus *[1 mark]* discolours the leaves of tobacco plants by stopping them from producing chloroplasts *[1 mark]*.

b) E.g. the influenza virus *[1 mark]* causes 'flu' *[1 mark]* / the HIV virus *[1 mark]* causes AIDS *[1 mark]*.

Page 8 — Enzymes

1 A *[1 mark]*

2 a) active site *[1 mark]*

b) The enzyme has been denatured by the high pH *[1 mark]*, which has changed its shape *[1 mark]*. This means that the substrate will no longer fit the active site *[1 mark]*, so the enzyme will no longer catalyse the reaction *[1 mark]*.

3 E.g. line 2 because this enzyme has a higher optimum temperature than the enzyme represented by line 1 *[1 mark]*. Also, the enzyme doesn't denature/the reaction doesn't stop until a higher temperature *[1 mark]*. The ability to function effectively at higher temperatures would be necessary for an enzyme found in a hot thermal vent *[1 mark]*.

Page 9 — Investigating Enzyme Activity

1 a) 36 °C, as this was the temperature at which the iodine solution stopped turning blue-black first *[1 mark]*, meaning the starch had been broken down the fastest *[1 mark]*.

b) E.g. the amylase was denatured by the high temperature, so the starch was not broken down *[1 mark]*.

c) Any two from: e.g. the concentration of starch solution / the concentration of amylase / the volume of starch and amylase solution added to the iodine / the volume of iodine solution in the wells / the pH of the starch and amylase solution *[2 marks]*.

d) E.g. test the solutions more frequently (e.g. every 10 seconds) *[1 mark]*. / Do more repeats of the experiment at 36 °C and at 37 °C *[1 mark]*.

e) E.g. by adding a buffer solution with a different pH level to each tube *[1 mark]*.

Page 10 — Diffusion

1 a) D *[1 mark]*

b) Diffusion will cause the oxygen concentration in the cell to decrease *[1 mark]*.

2 a)

[1 mark for dye particles spread out evenly]

b) The dye particles will move from an area of higher concentration (the drop of dye) to an area of lower concentration (the water) *[1 mark]*.

3   Z particles must be larger than X and Y particles *[1 mark]* because larger particles could not diffuse through the membrane *[1 mark]*.

Cell membranes are only partially permeable, so they won't allow larger molecules to pass through them.

Page 11 — Osmosis

1   C *[1 mark]*

2 a)   partially permeable membrane *[1 mark]*

Remember that osmosis always takes place across a partially permeable membrane.

  b)   The liquid level on side B will fall *[1 mark]*, because water will flow from the region of higher water concentration on side B to the region of lower water concentration on side A *[1 mark]*.

3 a)   The net movement of water would be into the body cells *[1 mark]* because the tissue fluid has a higher water concentration and the body cells have a lower water concentration *[1 mark]*.

  b)   The net movement of water molecules stops when there is an equal concentration of water molecules on either side of the membrane *[1 mark]*.

There needs to be a concentration gradient (i.e. a difference in the concentration of water molecules on either side of a membrane) for osmosis to take place.

Pages 12-13 — Diffusion and Osmosis Experiments

1 a)   diffusion *[1 mark]*

  b)   (835 + 825 + 842 + 838) ÷ 4 = **835 s** *[2 marks for correct answer, otherwise 1 mark for adding together 4 values and dividing by 4]*

  c)   As the size of the gelatine cube increases, the time taken for the cube to become yellow increases *[1 mark]*. This is because the bigger cubes have a smaller surface area to volume ratio *[1 mark]*, which decreases the rate of diffusion *[1 mark]*.

2 a)   E.g. they could measure the mass of each egg before putting it in its jar and measure each egg's mass again after one day. *[1 mark for stating what will be measured, 1 mark for stating a time period over which it will be measured]*

  b)   E.g. the egg in the weak sugar solution would lose mass and the egg in water would gain mass by the end of the experiment *[1 mark for describing a result in the weak sugar solution which suggests water has moved out of the egg, 1 mark for describing a result in the water which suggests water has moved into the egg]*

  c)   E.g. a third egg, weighed then placed back in the jar of vinegar *[1 mark]*.

3 a) i)   0.2 M — beaker B *[1 mark]* because the concentration of sucrose solution was the same on both sides of the membrane, so there has been no net movement of water molecules *[1 mark]*.

    ii) 0.0 M — beaker C *[1 mark]* because the concentration of water molecules was higher in the beaker than inside the Visking tubing, so water molecules moved into the Visking tubing by osmosis *[1 mark]*.

  b)   Any two from: e.g. the volume of sucrose solution put into the Visking tubing. / The volume of sucrose solution put into the beaker. / The temperature the beaker is kept at. / The size of the Visking tubing bag *[2 marks]*

  c)   E.g. by repeating the experiment *[1 mark]*.

Remember: repeats = (increased) reliability. It's as straightforward as that.

Page 14 — Active Transport

1 a)   Active transport is the movement of particles against a concentration gradient/from an area of lower concentration to an area of higher concentration *[1 mark]* using energy released in respiration *[1 mark]*.

  b)   Temperature — independent variable *[1 mark]* Concentration of potassium ion solution — control variable *[1 mark]* Initial size of seedling — control variable *[1 mark]* Rate of potassium ion uptake — dependent variable *[1 mark]*

  c) i) 7.5 arbitrary units *[1 mark]*

    ii) E.g. seedling A because there is more energy at higher temperatures *[1 mark]* so the potassium ions move faster, resulting in a faster rate of uptake *[1 mark]*.

  d)   It would have no effect *[1 mark]*.

Increasing a concentration gradient increases the rate of diffusion and osmosis but has no effect on the rate of active transport.

Section 2 — Human Nutrition

Page 15 — Biological Molecules

1   B *[1 mark]*

2 a)   (simple) sugars *[1 mark]*

  b)   amino acids *[1 mark]*

3   Bacterial species B because the clear zone around the bacteria indicates there is no lipid present in this area *[1 mark]*. This is because the lipase produced by the bacterial cells has broken it down into fatty acids and glycerol *[1 mark]*.

Page 16 — Food Tests

1 a)   He should add some Benedict's solution to each test tube using a pipette *[1 mark]*. He should then place the test tubes in a water bath set at 75 °C and leave them for 5 minutes *[1 mark]*. He should look out for a colour change and note which of a range of colours the solutions become *[1 mark]*.

  b)

	Tube 1	Tube 2	Tube 3	Tube 4
substance observed	yellow precipitate	blue solution	red precipitate	green precipitate
glucose concentration (M)	0.1	0	1	0.02

[1 mark]

The higher the concentration of glucose in the solution, the further the colour change goes along the following scale: blue — green — yellow — brick red. If no precipitate forms then there are no glucose molecules in the solution.

2   E.g. grind up a sample of the egg white using a pestle and mortar *[1 mark]*. Put the sample into a beaker and add some distilled water. Stir well with a glass rod to allow some of the food to dissolve in the water *[1 mark]*. Filter the mixture through a funnel lined with filter paper *[1 mark]*. Transfer 2 cm^3 of the filtered solution into a clean test tube *[1 mark]*. Add 2 cm^3 of Biuret solution and gently shake the test tube *[1 mark]*. If the food sample contains protein, the solution will change from blue to pink or purple. If no protein is present, the solution will stay bright blue *[1 mark]*.

Page 17 — A Balanced Diet

1 a)   B *[1 mark]*

  b) i) E.g. needed to make haemoglobin for healthy blood *[1 mark]*.

    ii) E.g. needed to make bones and teeth *[1 mark]*.

  c)   E.g. wholemeal bread / fruit *[1 mark]*

2 a)   Pregnant women need more energy than other women because they need to provide energy for their babies to develop *[1 mark]*.

  b)   E.g. teenagers need more energy than older people because they are still growing *[1 mark]*.

  c)   A diet that contains all the essential nutrients plus fibre *[1 mark]* in the right proportions *[1 mark]*. / A diet that contains carbohydrates, proteins, lipids, vitamins, minerals, water and fibre *[1 mark]* in the right proportions *[1 mark]*.

Page 18 — Energy From Food

1 a) The mass of the dried bean *[1 mark]*, the temperature of the water *[1 mark]*.

b) The change in temperature of the water *[1 mark]*.

c) Energy = 20 × 21 × 4.2 = **1764 J** *[1 mark]*

d) 1764 ÷ 0.7 = **2520 J/g** *[1 mark. Allow carry through of any answer from part b).]*

e) E.g. not all of the energy used to heat the water is retained by the water *[1 mark]* because it is lost to the surroundings instead *[1 mark]*.

f) E.g. she could insulate the boiling tube (to reduce heat loss) *[1 mark]*.

Page 19 — Enzymes and Digestion

1

Enzyme	Function
proteases	convert proteins into **amino acids**
amylase	converts starch into maltose
maltase	converts maltose into glucose
lipases	convert lipids into fatty acids and **glycerol**

[5 marks]

2 a) i) bile *[1 mark]*

ii) Produced: liver *[1 mark]*
Acts: small intestine *[1 mark]*

iii) The enzymes in the small intestine (where the bile/fluid acts) work best in alkaline conditions *[1 mark]*. The alkaline bile/fluid neutralises the acid from the stomach and makes conditions alkaline, so the enzymes can work *[1 mark]*.

b) Bile emulsifies fat/breaks fat down into tiny droplets *[1 mark]*. This gives a larger surface area for lipases to work on and so the fat is digested more quickly *[1 mark]*. The gallstones could block the bile ducts and prevent bile from entering the small intestine *[1 mark]*. If so, any fat may be digested more slowly, possibly causing problems *[1 mark]*.

Page 20 — The Alimentary Canal

1 a) It produces protease, amylase and lipase enzymes *[1 mark]* and releases these into the small intestine *[1 mark]*.

b)

Function	Label letter
Pummels the food, and produces the protease enzyme pepsin.	E
Contains salivary glands which produce amylase.	A
Where nutrients are absorbed from food.	F

[3 marks]

c) small intestine *[1 mark]*

2 a) Peristalsis squeezes balls of food/boluses through the gut *[1 mark]* to prevent it from becoming clogged up with food *[1 mark]*.

b) Food passes through the colon too quickly *[1 mark]*, which means that excess water is not absorbed from the food, resulting in excess water in the faeces/diarrhoea *[1 mark]*.

Section 3 — Plant Nutrition and Transport

Page 21 — Photosynthesis

1 delivers water and nutrients to every part of the leaf — E *[1 mark]*
helps to reduce water loss by evaporation — A *[1 mark]*
where most of the chloroplasts in the leaf are located, to maximise the amount of light they receive — B *[1 mark]*
allows carbon dioxide to diffuse directly into the leaf — D *[1 mark]*

2 a) Photosynthesis involves the conversion of light energy to chemical energy *[1 mark]*, which is stored in glucose *[1 mark]*.

b) i) carbon dioxide + water → glucose + oxygen
[1 mark for carbon dioxide + water on the left-hand side of the equation, 1 mark for glucose + oxygen on the right.]

ii) $6CO_2 + 6H_2O \rightarrow C_6H_{12}O_6 + 6O_2$
[1 mark for $6CO_2 + 6H_2O$ on the left-hand side of the equation, 1 mark for $C_6H_{12}O_6 + 6O_2$ on the right. Allow 1 mark if the correct symbols are used, but the equation isn't correctly balanced.]

Pages 22-23 — Rate of Photosynthesis

1 a) The faster the rate of photosynthesis, the faster the growth rate of grass *[1 mark]*. / The lower the rate of photosynthesis, the lower the growth rate of grass *[1 mark]*.

b) The temperature will be lower in winter than in summer *[1 mark]* and the light intensity will be lower in winter than in summer *[1 mark]*. Both of these factors will reduce the rate of photosynthesis and therefore the growth rate of the grass *[1 mark]*.

2 a) At low light intensities, increasing the CO_2 concentration has no effect *[1 mark]*, but at higher light intensities, increasing the concentration of CO_2 increases the maximum rate of photosynthesis *[1 mark]*.

b) The rate of photosynthesis does not continue to increase because temperature or the level of carbon dioxide becomes the limiting factor *[1 mark]*.

3 a)

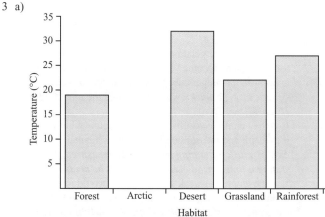

[1 mark for a bar chart covering at least half of the grid, 1 mark for bars drawn with lines, 1 mark for correctly labelling the axes, including the correct units for temperature, 1 mark for correctly plotted data.]

b) The Arctic *[1 mark]*. The temperatures are extremely low there *[1 mark]*, so the rate of photosynthesis will be lower *[1 mark]* because the enzymes needed for photosynthesis will be working very slowly *[1 mark]*.

c) E.g. because plants growing close to the ground in a dense rainforest will receive less light than taller plants *[1 mark]* and a low light intensity limits the rate of photosynthesis *[1 mark]*.

Pages 24-25 — Photosynthesis Experiments

1 a) That photosynthesis requires carbon dioxide *[1 mark]*.

b) So you know that any changes in the plant's growth are caused by the lack of carbon dioxide and not another factor *[1 mark]*.

2 a) The chlorophyll was removed from the leaf *[1 mark]*.

b) That starch is present in the leaf *[1 mark]*.

c) The green parts of the leaf would turn blue-black *[1 mark]* and the white part of the leaf would turn brown *[1 mark]*. This is because the green parts of the leaf contain chlorophyll and so they will be able to photosynthesise and produce starch *[1 mark]*. The white part of the leaf does not contain chlorophyll, so it will not be able to photosynthesise or produce starch *[1 mark]*.

Remember, photosynthesis produces glucose, which is stored in the leaves as starch.

3 a)

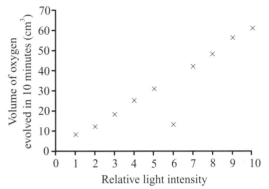

[1 mark for a graph covering at least half of the grid, 1 mark for correctly labelling the axes, including use of the correct units for volume of oxygen, 1 mark for correctly plotted points.]

b) i) 6 *[1 mark]*

ii) E.g. she might have measured the volume of oxygen evolved in less time than 10 minutes *[1 mark]*. / She might have accidentally used a lower light intensity *[1 mark]*. / She might have measured the volume of oxygen evolved wrongly *[1 mark]*.

c) The rate of photosynthesis increases as light intensity increases *[1 mark]*. / There is a positive correlation between rate of photosynthesis and light intensity *[1 mark]*.

4 E.g. take two plants of the same type. Grow one plant without any light for a week (e.g. in a dark cupboard). Grow the other plant in bright light for a week (e.g. in a cupboard under artificial lights). Keep both plants at the same temperature and give them the same amount of water. Keep the carbon dioxide concentration for both plants the same too. After one week, take a leaf from each plant and test it for starch using iodine solution. Record the results. Repeat the experiment at least twice.

[1 mark for stating that one or more plants will be grown without light and one or more will be grown with light, 1 mark for stating that plants should be the same type, 1 mark for describing one control variable, e.g. temperature, 1 mark for describing a second control variable, e.g. water, 1 mark for stating what will be measured, e.g. starch production, 1 mark for stating how it will be measured, e.g. using the iodine test, 1 mark for stating that repeats should be carried out. Maximum 6 marks available.]

Page 26 — Minerals for Healthy Growth

1 Nitrate ions are needed for making amino acids *[1 mark]*, which the tomato plants need to grow *[1 mark]*.

2 a) E.g. to act as controls. / To allow comparison between them and the plants that were grown without magnesium *[1 mark]*.

b) The plants are lacking in magnesium and magnesium is needed to make chlorophyll (the pigment that makes plant leaves green) *[1 mark]*.

c) i) The magnesium-deficient plants had a lower total dry mass than those grown with a complete mineral supply *[1 mark]*.

ii) The magnesium-deficient plants are unable to produce chlorophyll, which is needed for photosynthesis *[1 mark]*. If photosynthesis is reduced, plant growth will also be reduced *[1 mark]* and the plants will gain less mass *[1 mark]*.

Page 27 — Transport in Plants

1 C *[1 mark]*

2 a) Osmosis *[1 mark]*. Water moves from a higher concentration in the soil to a lower concentration in the root hair cell *[1 mark]*.

b) E.g. they have a large surface area *[1 mark]*.

3 In unicellular organisms, substances can diffuse directly into and out of the cell (across the cell membrane) *[1 mark]*. The rate of diffusion is quick because of the short distances substances have to travel *[1 mark]*. But in multicellular organisms, diffusion across the outer surface would be too slow to reach every cell in the organism's body *[1 mark]*. So multicellular organisms need transport systems to move substances to and from individual cells quickly *[1 mark]*.

Page 28 — Transpiration

1 a) E.g. the evaporation (and diffusion) of water from a plant's surface *[1 mark]*.

b) 9 a.m. *[1 mark]*

c) Any one from: e.g. day 2 was colder, so the water evaporated/diffused more slowly. / Day 2 was less windy, so the water vapour was carried away more slowly. / Day 2 was wetter/more humid, so there was a smaller diffusion gradient, so the water diffused more slowly. / The light intensity was lower on day 2, so fewer stomata were open to allow water vapour to escape. *[1 mark for reason, 1 mark for explanation]*

d) At night the light intensity is low *[1 mark]* so the stomata close, allowing less water vapour to escape *[1 mark]*.

2 a) E.g.

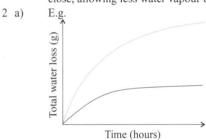

[1 mark for a curve drawn lower than that on the hot, dry day]

b) As it gets warmer the rate of transpiration increases because the water particles have more energy to evaporate and diffuse out of the stomata *[1 mark]*.

Page 29 — Measuring Transpiration

1 a) 10 + 11 + 9 = 30, 30 ÷ 3 = **10%** *[2 marks for correct answer, otherwise 1 mark for adding together 3 percentages and dividing by 3.]*

b) The movement of air from the fan sweeps away water vapour, maintaining a low concentration of water outside the leaf *[1 mark]* and increasing the rate at which water is lost through diffusion *[1 mark]*. This means that the plants next to the fan would lose more water (and therefore more mass) than the plants in a still room in the same amount of time *[1 mark]*.

c) To make her results more reliable *[1 mark]*.

d) E.g. you could spray a little water into three clear plastic bags to increase the humidity *[1 mark]* before sealing each bag around a separate new basil plant *[1 mark]*.

If you've thought of another sensible way to increase or decrease the humidity around the plants, you'd still get the mark in the exam.

Section 4 — Respiration and Gas Exchange

Page 30 — Respiration

1 a) To transfer energy from glucose. / To produce ATP which provides energy for cells *[1 mark]*.

b) Any two from: e.g. aerobic respiration uses oxygen, anaerobic respiration does not. / Glucose is only partially broken down during anaerobic respiration, but is broken down fully during aerobic respiration. / Anaerobic respiration produces lactic acid, aerobic respiration does not. / Anaerobic respiration transfers less energy/produces less ATP than aerobic respiration. *[2 marks]*

c) B *[1 mark]*

2 a) E.g. during vigorous exercise *[1 mark]*.

b) glucose → lactic acid *[1 mark]*

c) E.g. it transfers much less energy/produces fewer molecules of ATP (per glucose molecule) than aerobic respiration *[1 mark]*. Lactic acid builds up in the muscles, causing pain/cramp *[1 mark]*.

d) ethanol *[1 mark]*, carbon dioxide/CO$_2$ *[1 mark]*

Page 31 — Investigating Respiration

1 a) Tube A: the bromothymol blue indicator has changed colour from green to yellow *[1 mark]*. This is because the beetle has respired and produced carbon dioxide *[1 mark]*.
Tube B: the bromothymol blue indicator has not changed colour/is still green *[1 mark]* because no respiration has taken place, so no carbon dioxide has been produced *[1 mark]*.

b) To act as a control / to show that the colour change in the indicator solution only happened in the presence of a living/respiring organism *[1 mark]*.

2 E.g. divide dried peas of the same variety into two batches. Soak one batch until the peas germinate. Boil one batch to kill the peas so they can't respire/to act as a control. Place the two batches into separate vacuum flasks with thermometers and seal the flasks with cotton wool so that air/oxygen can still enter the flasks, allowing the peas to respire aerobically. The vacuum flask/cotton wool insulates the peas against changes in the external temperature. Record the temperature of each flask at regular intervals for one week. Repeat the experiment at least three times using the same mass of peas each time. The germinating peas will respire and transfer energy by heat so the temperature of this flask should be higher than the control flask.
[1 mark for including a control (e.g. boiled peas), 1 mark for stating the organisms should be of the same type/size, 1 mark for stating that the investigation should be repeated, 1 mark for stating that the temperature should be measured, 1 mark for saying how the temperature should be measured, 1 mark for controlling one variable (e.g. external temperature / mass of organisms used), 1 mark for controlling a second variable. Maximum of 6 marks available.]

Pages 32-34 — Gas Exchange — Flowering Plants

1 a) i) A: oxygen / water vapour *[1 mark]*
B: carbon dioxide *[1 mark]*
ii) diffusion *[1 mark]*
b) i) photosynthesis *[1 mark]*
ii) respiration *[1 mark]*

2 Leaves are broad *[1 mark]* so there is a large surface area for diffusion of gases *[1 mark]*. Leaves are thin *[1 mark]* so gases only have to travel/diffuse a short distance to reach cells where they're used *[1 mark]*. Air spaces in the leaf *[1 mark]* increase the surface area for gas exchange/allow gases to move easily between cells *[1 mark]*.

3 At night, when light intensity is low *[1 mark]*, respiration takes place but photosynthesis does not *[1 mark]*. This means the plant produces carbon dioxide in respiration, but doesn't use up any in photosynthesis *[1 mark]*. So there is a higher concentration of carbon dioxide inside the leaf than outside of the leaf *[1 mark]*, and it diffuses out of the leaf *[1 mark]*.

4 a) Gas A is carbon dioxide. As the light intensity increases, the carbon dioxide concentration should decrease *[1 mark]* because the plant uses up more carbon dioxide in photosynthesis *[1 mark]*.
Gas B is oxygen. As light intensity increases, the oxygen concentration should increase *[1 mark]* because more photosynthesis occurs and more oxygen is produced *[1 mark]*.

b)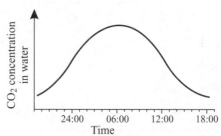

[1 mark for bell shaped curve with CO$_2$ concentration gradually increasing then gradually decreasing, 1 mark for a maximum at or shortly after 6 am.]

The CO$_2$ concentration should be highest at the end of the night (6 am) because when it is dark the CO$_2$ produced by respiration is not used up in photosynthesis. The CO$_2$ concentration should be lowest at the end of the day (6 pm) because photosynthesis during daylight hours has gradually used up the CO$_2$ in the water.

5 a) To prevent gas exchange with the surrounding air *[1 mark]*.

b) To make sure that any change in the hydrogen-carbonate indicator is due to processes occurring in the leaves *[1 mark]*.

c) Tube A: no/little change in colour of the hydrogen-carbonate indicator *[1 mark]*. Some light is available, so the rates of photosynthesis and respiration roughly balance and the CO$_2$ concentration in the tube remains the same/similar *[1 mark]*.
Tube B: hydrogen-carbonate indicator turns yellow *[1 mark]*. Foil blocks out all light, so the CO$_2$ produced by respiration is not used up in photosynthesis. This means that the CO$_2$ concentration in the tube increases *[1 mark]*.
Tube C: hydrogen-carbonate indicator turns purple *[1 mark]*. The rate of photosynthesis will be high because of the bright light, so the leaf takes up more CO$_2$ than it produces through respiration and the CO$_2$ concentration in the tube decreases *[1 mark]*.

Page 35 — The Respiratory System and Ventilation

1 a) E.g.

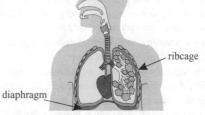

[1 mark for a label pointing to the diaphragm, 1 mark for a label pointing to the ribcage].

b) bronchiole *[1 mark]*
c) Around/surrounding the lungs *[1 mark]*.
d) the alveoli *[1 mark]*

2

Event	Order
Pressure in the lungs decreases	3
Intercostal muscles and diaphragm contract	1
Air is drawn into the lungs	4
Thorax volume increases	2

[3 marks for all answers in the correct order, 2 marks for three answers in the correct order, 1 mark for two answers in the correct order.]

Page 36 — Investigating Breathing

1   The limewater in boiling tube B will turn cloudy *[1 mark]* because the exhaled air that passes through the limewater in tube B contains carbon dioxide *[1 mark]*.

2   E.g. the person being tested should first sit still for 5 minutes. The number of breaths they take in one minute should then be recorded. These time periods should be measured with a stopwatch. The same person should then run on a treadmill for 4 minutes. The number of breaths they take in one minute should then be recorded immediately. Repeats should be carried out using the same time periods, the same intensity of exercise (e.g. by setting the same speed on the treadmill), and at the same temperature.

[1 mark for including a control (i.e. recording the breathing rate at rest), 1 mark for stating that the same person should do the rest and exercise tests, 1 mark for stating that the breathing rate should be measured, 1 mark for saying how the breathing rate should be measured, 1 mark for stating that the investigation should be repeated, 1 mark for controlling one variable (e.g. length of rest/exercise periods / intensity of exercise / temperature at which experiment takes place), 1 mark for controlling a second variable. Maximum of 6 marks available.]

Page 37 — Gas Exchange — Humans

1 a)   The blood in the capillary has just returned to the lungs from the rest of the body, so contains a low concentration of oxygen *[1 mark]*. The alveolus contains air that has just been breathed in, so it has a high concentration of oxygen *[1 mark]*. So oxygen diffuses out of the alveolus and into the capillary *[1 mark]*.

   b)   Any two from: e.g. they have thin outer walls *[1 mark]* so gases don't have to diffuse far/there's a short diffusion pathway *[1 mark]*. / They have a moist lining *[1 mark]* which gases can dissolve in *[1 mark]*. / They have a good blood supply *[1 mark]* to maintain a high concentration gradient *[1 mark]*. / They have permeable walls *[1 mark]* to allow gases to diffuse easily *[1 mark]*.

2 a)   The percentage of male smokers has been decreasing since 1950 *[1 mark]*. The percentage of female smokers increased between 1950 and 1970, then decreased from 1970 to 2000 *[1 mark]*.

   b)   E.g. increased awareness of the health risks of smoking *[1 mark]*.

   c)   Any two from: e.g. smoking damages the walls of the alveoli *[1 mark]*, reducing the area for gas exchange/leading to diseases like emphysema *[1 mark]*. / Tar damages cilia in the trachea/lungs *[1 mark]*, leading to the build up of mucus/ making chest infections more likely *[1 mark]*. / Tar irritates the bronchi/bronchioles *[1 mark]*, leading to excess mucus production/a smoker's cough/chronic bronchitis *[1 mark]*. / Carbon monoxide reduces the oxygen carrying capacity of the blood *[1 mark]*. This makes the heart rate increase, which can lead to high blood pressure and an increased risk of coronary heart disease/heart attacks *[1 mark]*. / Tobacco contains carcinogens *[1 mark]* which can lead to cancers (e.g. lung cancer) *[1 mark]*.

Section 5 — Blood and Organs

Page 38 — Functions of the Blood

1 a)   red blood cells *[1 mark]*, white blood cells *[1 mark]*, platelets *[1 mark]*

   b)   Any two from: e.g. digested food / carbon dioxide / hormones *[2 marks]*.

2 a)   It is biconcave *[1 mark]* which gives it a large surface area for absorbing and releasing oxygen *[1 mark]*.

   b)   E.g. it contains haemoglobin *[1 mark]* which reacts with oxygen so red blood cells can carry it around the body *[1 mark]*. / It has no nucleus *[1 mark]* so there is space for more haemoglobin and so more oxygen *[1 mark]*.

3 a)   E.g. platelets *[1 mark]*

Platelets are the component of the blood that are involved in blood clotting, so if a condition means that people's blood doesn't clot properly it's likely that it's something to do with the platelets.

   b)   Because the blood does not clot properly, the cut will not seal quickly *[1 mark]*. As a result, the person might lose more blood from the cut *[1 mark]*. They are also more at risk of infection because microorganisms could enter the cut *[1 mark]*.

Page 39 — White Blood Cells and Immunity

1 a)   Some white blood cells/phagocytes can engulf pathogens *[1 mark]* and digest them *[1 mark]*.

   b)   Antibodies are produced by certain white blood cells/ lymphocytes *[1 mark]*. They attach to specific antigens on the surface of the pathogen *[1 mark]* and mark the pathogen for destruction by other white blood cells *[1 mark]*.

2   When vaccinated, child A was given dead or inactive rubella pathogens *[1 mark]*. These would have had antigens on their surface and so would cause lymphocytes to start producing antibodies *[1 mark]*. Memory cells would also have been produced and remained in the blood *[1 mark]*. When child A was exposed to the virus, the memory cells made the specific antibodies more quickly/in greater quantities, so child A didn't become ill *[1 mark]*. Child B did not have these memory cells so when they were infected by the virus, they became ill *[1 mark]*.

Page 40 — Blood Vessels

1 a)   Arteries carry blood away from the heart *[1 mark]* and veins carry blood back to the heart *[1 mark]*.

   b)   Any two from: e.g. the vein has a bigger lumen/thinner wall/ valves. / The artery has a smaller lumen/thicker wall/no valves. *[2 marks]*

To answer this question, you need to think about how the structure of veins and arteries differ — and how you could tell them apart by just looking at them.

   c)   The artery is more elastic *[1 mark]*. Arteries have more elastic fibres to allow them to expand as they carry blood under high pressure *[1 mark]*.

2 a)   Any two from, e.g. some food molecules, oxygen, carbon dioxide *[2 marks]*

   b)   E.g. capillaries are very small *[1 mark]* so they can carry blood close to any cell *[1 mark]*. They have permeable walls *[1 mark]* so substances can diffuse in and out of them *[1 mark]*. Their walls are only one cell thick *[1 mark]* to increase the rate of diffusion by decreasing the distance over which it happens *[1 mark]*.

Pages 41-42 — The Heart

1 a)   A: aorta *[1 mark]*
       B: vena cava *[1 mark]*
       C: left atrium *[1 mark]*

   b)   To pump blood out of the heart *[1 mark]*.

   c)   To prevent the backflow of blood *[1 mark]*.

   d)   pulmonary vein *[1 mark]*

2 a)   The left ventricle pumps blood to the whole body *[1 mark]* so it has a very muscular wall which is thicker *[1 mark]*. The right ventricle only pumps blood to the lungs *[1 mark]* so it doesn't have as much muscle, and so it is thinner *[1 mark]*.

   b)   Deoxygenated blood arrives at the heart through the vena cava *[1 mark]* and enters the right atrium *[1 mark]*. The blood is then pumped into the right ventricle *[1 mark]*, which contracts to pump it to the lungs through the pulmonary artery *[1 mark]*.

3 a)   Friend 2 *[1 mark]*

b) Any two from: e.g. his friends should run the same distance *[1 mark]*. / His friends should run at the same speed *[1 mark]*. / He should conduct all the tests at the same temperature *[1 mark]*. / He should measure the pulse rates of his friends over the same time period *[1 mark]*.

c) Because the body/muscles need(s) more energy *[1 mark]* and so respire(s) more, which requires more oxygen *[1 mark]*.

4 a) The cat sensed a threat from the dog so its adrenal glands secreted adrenaline *[1 mark]*. Adrenaline binds to specific receptors in the heart *[1 mark]*, causing the cardiac muscle to contract more frequently, so the cat's heart rate increased *[1 mark]*.

b) By increasing the oxygen supply to the tissues *[1 mark]*.

Page 43 — Circulation and Coronary Heart Disease

1

Structure	Letter
pulmonary artery	B
hepatic artery	F
vena cava	C
kidneys	H
aorta	E
hepatic portal vein	G

[1 mark for each correct answer]

2 a) E.g. smoking increases blood pressure, which can cause damage to the inside of the coronary arteries / chemicals in cigarette smoke can cause damage to the inside of the coronary arteries *[1 mark]*. The damage makes it more likely that fatty deposits will form, which cause a narrowing of the coronary arteries *[1 mark]*.

b) E.g. cut down on foods high in saturated fat *[1 mark]* / exercise regularly *[1 mark]*.

Page 44 — Excretion — The Kidneys

1 a) E.g. lungs / skin *[1 mark]*.

b)

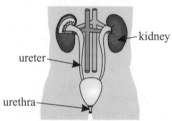

[1 mark for each correct answer — either kidney and either ureter can be labelled for the mark]

2 a) Bowman's capsule *[1 mark]*

b) i) As the blood flows from the renal artery into the glomerulus *[1 mark]* a high pressure builds up *[1 mark]*, which squeezes/ filters small molecules out of the blood into the Bowman's capsule to form the glomerular filtrate *[1 mark]*.

ii) C *[1 mark]*

Page 45 — Osmoregulation — The Kidneys

1 a) E.g. the maintenance of a balance between water coming into the body and water going out of the body *[1 mark]*.

b) urine *[1 mark]*

c) i) B *[1 mark]*

ii) pituitary gland *[1 mark]*

2 As the runner ran, she sweated, resulting in water loss and less water in her blood *[1 mark]*. Her brain detected the decreased water content of her blood *[1 mark]* and instructed the pituitary gland to release ADH (anti-diuretic hormone) into the blood *[1 mark]*. The ADH made the collecting ducts of the nephrons more permeable *[1 mark]* so that more water could be reabsorbed back into the blood *[1 mark]*, resulting in less water being released in her urine, so her urine was more concentrated and appeared darker in colour *[1 mark]*.

Section 6 — Coordination and Response

Pages 46-47 — The Nervous System and Responding to Stimuli

1 a) E.g. so they can respond to the changes in order to avoid danger/increase their chances of survival *[1 mark]*.

b) receptors *[1 mark]*

c) Stimulus: sight of food *[1 mark]*
Sense organ: the eye *[1 mark]*
Effectors: muscle cells *[1 mark]*

d) hormonal system *[1 mark]*

2 a) brain *[1 mark]*, spinal cord *[1 mark]*

b) sensory neurone *[1 mark]*

c) Because information is transmitted using high speed electrical impulses *[1 mark]*.

3 a) E.g. the scientists can't draw this conclusion as they have only studied five body parts *[1 mark]*, so another body part may have more pressure receptors *[1 mark]*.

b) Receptor cells in the lip detected the stimulus/pins *[1 mark]* and sent electrical impulses along (sensory) neurones/ nerves to the central nervous system *[1 mark]*. The central nervous system then sent electrical impulses along (motor) neurones/nerves to effector cells/muscles *[1 mark]*, which responded by contracting, moving her head away from the pins *[1 mark]*.

c) It reduces the validity *[1 mark]* because the scientists may have been applying different pressures, meaning that the experiment was not a fair test *[1 mark]*.

d) Because the information from the pressure receptors in the knee may be unable to be transmitted through the spinal cord to the brain *[1 mark]*.

Page 48 — Reflexes

1 a) C *[1 mark]*

b) E.g. to prevent injury *[1 mark]*.

2 a) X: sensory neurone *[1 mark]*
Y: relay neurone *[1 mark]*
Z: motor neurone *[1 mark]*

b) The effectors are muscle cells *[1 mark]* and they respond by contracting (which causes the man to drop the plate) *[1 mark]*.

Page 49 — The Eye

1 a) A: cornea *[1 mark]*
B: pupil *[1 mark]*

b) To control the diameter of the pupil/the amount of light entering the eye *[1 mark]*.

2 a) B, because the pupil has contracted in this eye *[1 mark]* to stop too much light entering the eye *[1 mark]*.

b) Reflex responses happen very quickly/are automatic *[1 mark]* so the eye can adjust quickly to prevent the retina being damaged by bright light *[1 mark]*.

3 a) The ciliary muscles relax *[1 mark]*, allowing the suspensory ligaments to pull tight *[1 mark]*, which results in the lens becoming thinner/less rounded *[1 mark]*.

b) If the lens cannot form a rounded shape, light from nearby objects won't be bent/refracted enough to be focused on the retina *[1 mark]*. This means that people with presbyopia will be unable to focus on nearby objects *[1 mark]*.

Page 50 — Hormones

1 a)

Hormone	Source	Effect(s)
Oestrogen	Ovaries	Controls the menstrual cycle and promotes female secondary sexual characteristics.
Adrenaline	Adrenal glands	Increases heart rate, blood flow to muscles and blood sugar level.
Progesterone	Ovaries	Maintains the uterus lining.

[1 mark for each correct answer]

b) i) testosterone *[1 mark]*, testes *[1 mark]*
   ii) The role of insulin is to help control blood sugar level *[1 mark]*. It stimulates the liver to turn glucose into glycogen *[1 mark]*.
c) It increases the permeability of the kidney tubules to water *[1 mark]*.
2 Nervous responses are very fast and hormonal responses are slower *[1 mark]*. Nerves use electrical impulses/signals, while hormones use chemical signals *[1 mark]*. Nervous responses usually act for a short time while hormonal responses last for longer *[1 mark]*. Nerves act on a very precise area whereas hormones act on a more general area *[1 mark]*.

Page 51 — Homeostasis

1 a) The maintenance of a constant internal environment *[1 mark]*.
b) i) Through his skin as sweat *[1 mark]*.
      Via the lungs in his breath *[1 mark]*.
   ii) It is very concentrated *[1 mark]* because he has lost a lot of water in his sweat/breath, so loses less in his urine *[1 mark]*.
c) E.g. it is a cooler day so he sweats less. / He drank more water before/during the ride *[1 mark]*.
2 a) The optimum temperature for many enzymes controlling reactions in the human body is 37 °C *[1 mark]*.
b) The woman's brain is sensitive to the blood temperature in the brain *[1 mark]* and it also receives messages/impulses from temperature receptors in the skin *[1 mark]*. Based on the signals from these receptors, the woman's central nervous system sends signals/impulses to the necessary effectors to make sure her body stays at a safe temperature *[1 mark]*.

Page 52 — More on Homeostasis

1 a) i) vasoconstriction *[1 mark]*
   ii) It means that less blood flows near the surface *[1 mark]*, so less energy is transferred to the surroundings, which helps to keep the body warm *[1 mark]*.
b) Sweat glands respond by producing very little sweat *[1 mark]*, because sweat transfers heat from the body to the environment when it evaporates *[1 mark]*.
2 a) Skin temperature will increase, so the sweat glands will respond by producing lots of sweat *[1 mark]*. Drinking water will help to restore the water balance in the body *[1 mark]*.
b) Any two from: the blood vessels close to the skin's surface would widen/dilate / vasodilation would occur *[1 mark]*, which allows more blood to flow near to the surface of the skin *[1 mark]* so more energy can be transferred to the surroundings, cooling the body *[1 mark]*. / Lots of sweat is produced *[1 mark]* so that when it evaporates *[1 mark]*, it transfers energy from the body to the environment, cooling the body *[1 mark]*. / Hairs on the surface of the skin lie flat *[1 mark]* to avoid trapping an insulating layer of air *[1 mark]* which would keep the body warm *[1 mark]*.

Pages 53-54 — Responses in Plants

1 a) i) A growth response away from gravity *[1 mark]*.
   ii) The shoot *[1 mark]*.
b) i) The root will grow down again *[1 mark]*.
   ii) D *[1 mark]*
2 a) The plant grows towards the light to maximise light absorption for photosynthesis in order to increase its chance of survival *[1 mark]*.
b) As the shoot is exposed to light, more auxin accumulates in the side that's in the shade than the side that's in the light *[1 mark]*. This makes the cells grow/elongate faster on the shaded side *[1 mark]*, so the shoot bends towards the light *[1 mark]*.
3 A plant's roots are positively geotropic *[1 mark]*, meaning they grow towards gravity / down into the soil *[1 mark]* so they're able to absorb more nutrients / have good access to nutrients *[1 mark]*.

4 a) the tip *[1 mark]*
b) Shoot B grew straight upwards / did not bend *[1 mark]*. This is because the tip of the shoot was not exposed to light *[1 mark]*, which is the stimulus needed for phototropism to occur *[1 mark]*.
c) Any two from: e.g. the shoots should have been from the same type of plant. / Each shoot should have been the same distance from the light source. / The light source should have been the same intensity for each shoot. / Each shoot should have been exposed to the light stimulus for the same amount of time. / Each shoot should have been left to grow at the same temperature. / Each shoot should have been given the same amount of nutrients/water. *[2 marks]*
d) E.g. it's likely that none of the shoots would have bent / all of the shoots would have grown straight up *[1 mark]* as auxin/ the hormone responsible for the response is produced in the tips *[1 mark]*.

Section 7 — Reproduction and Inheritance

Page 55 — DNA, Genes and Chromosomes

1 a) the nucleus *[1 mark]*
b) i) They have two copies of each chromosome *[1 mark]*.
   ii) 46 *[1 mark]*
c) C *[1 mark]*
2 a) Each gene codes for a specific protein *[1 mark]*, and proteins determine inherited characteristics *[1 mark]*.
b) There are different/alternative versions of the same gene, called alleles *[1 mark]*, that give different versions of a characteristic *[1 mark]*. The two kittens must have different versions/alleles of the gene for fur length, meaning one is long-haired and the other is short-haired *[1 mark]*.

Pages 56-57 — Protein Synthesis

1 C *[1 mark]*
Each amino acid is coded for by a set of three bases. There are 14 bases in total — that's four sets of three bases with two left over.
2 a) C *[1 mark]*
mRNA contains almost the same bases as DNA. The only difference is T (thymine) is replaced by U (uracil).
b) B *[1 mark]*
c) nucleus *[1 mark]*
d) (complementary) base pairing *[1 mark]*
e) To bring amino acids to the ribosome in the correct order *[1 mark]*.
f) To carry the coding information from DNA in the nucleus *[1 mark]*, to the ribosomes in the cytoplasm (where protein synthesis takes place) *[1 mark]*.
3 Each of these proteins is coded for by a different gene *[1 mark]*. Each gene has a different sequence of bases *[1 mark]* that code for a different number and order of amino acids *[1 mark]*, which produce different proteins with different functions *[1 mark]*.
4 RNA polymerase binds to the region of non-coding DNA in front of the gene *[1 mark]*. The two DNA strands unzip and the RNA polymerase moves along one of the strands, using the coding DNA in the gene as a template to make mRNA *[1 mark]*. Base pairing ensures that the mRNA is complementary to the gene *[1 mark]*. Once made, the mRNA molecule moves out of the nucleus and joins to a ribosome in the cytoplasm *[1 mark]*. tRNA molecules bring amino acids to the ribosome — anticodons on the tRNA pair up with complementary codons in the mRNA to ensure that amino acids are brought to the ribosome in the correct order *[1 mark]*. The ribosome joins the amino acids together to make a protein *[1 mark]*.

Page 58 — Asexual Reproduction and Mitosis

1 a) asexual reproduction *[1 mark]*
  b) They will be identical *[1 mark]*.
  c) E.g. growth / repair of tissues *[1 mark]*
2 a) The amount of DNA is doubling *[1 mark]* because each new cell needs to have a complete set of chromosomes *[1 mark]*.
  b) The two new cells separate *[1 mark]*.
  c) two *[1 mark]*

Page 59 — Sexual Reproduction and Meiosis

1 a) i) three *[1 mark]*
   ii) four *[1 mark]*
When a diploid cell undergoes meiosis, four haploid gametes are produced — it doesn't matter whether you're talking about human cells or mosquito cells.
  b) Meiosis produces gametes that are genetically different to each other *[1 mark]*. A male gamete and a female gamete then combine at random at fertilisation *[1 mark]*, so the offspring inherits a random mixture of chromosomes from both parents *[1 mark]*.
2 a)

[1 mark]

The left-hand diagram in the question shows a cell containing two pairs of chromosomes just before it undergoes meiosis. The first division causes these pairs to split up so that the two new cells only contain one chromosome from each pair. In the second division the chromosome in each cell is pulled apart so that each of the four gametes ends up containing only one chromosome arm.
  b) It's needed to produce cells/gametes with half the number of chromosomes in the body cells *[1 mark]* so that when two gametes fuse at fertilisation, chromosomes from the mother and father can pair up *[1 mark]* and the zygote ends up with the full number of chromosomes *[1 mark]*.

Page 60 — Sexual Reproduction in Plants

1 a) Pollen grains from an anther *[1 mark]* are transferred to a stigma *[1 mark]*, so that male gametes can fertilise female gametes *[1 mark]*.
  b) Sexual reproduction involving only one plant / the transfer of pollen from an anther to a stigma on the same plant *[1 mark]*.
2 a) X: Filament *[1 mark]*. It supports the anther *[1 mark]*.
   Y: Ovary *[1 mark]*. It contains the female gametes/eggs *[1 mark]*.
  b) Flower B because e.g. long filaments hang the anthers outside the flower *[1 mark]*, so that a lot of pollen gets blown away *[1 mark]* / the large, feathery stigmas *[1 mark]* are efficient at catching pollen drifting past in the air *[1 mark]*.
  c) Any two from: e.g. brightly coloured petals to attract insects / scented flowers/nectaries/produce nectar to attract insects / large, sticky pollen grains that stick easily to insects / a sticky stigma to collect pollen from insects *[2 marks]*.

Page 61 — Fertilisation and Germination in Plants

1 a) A pollen tube grows out of the pollen grain and down through the style to the ovary and into the ovule *[1 mark]*. A nucleus from the male gamete moves down the tube to join with a female gamete in the ovule *[1 mark]*. The nuclei fuse together during fertilisation to make a zygote *[1 mark]*, which divides by mitosis to form an embryo *[1 mark]*. The fertilised female gamete forms a seed *[1 mark]*.
  b) From food reserves stored within the seed *[1 mark]*.
2 a) Because oxygen is needed for germination *[1 mark]* and oxygen was removed from the air in flask A by the sodium pyrogallate solution *[1 mark]*.
  b) E.g. normally, after seeds have produced green leaves, they can start to obtain energy through photosynthesis *[1 mark]*. But in flask B, sodium hydroxide removed the carbon dioxide from the air, so photosynthesis couldn't occur *[1 mark]*. The seedlings had used up their food reserves, so there was no energy available for growth *[1 mark]*.

Page 62 — Investigating Seed Germination

1 a) Tube C, as it has been kept at room temperature and has a supply of water and oxygen *[1 mark]*.
  b) Tube A: the seeds will not have germinated *[1 mark]* because oxygen is not present *[1 mark]*.
   Tube B: the seeds will not have germinated *[1 mark]* because water is not present *[1 mark]*.
   Tube C: the seeds will be germinating *[1 mark]* because oxygen and water are present and they have been kept at a suitable temperature *[1 mark]*.
  c) It stops the enzymes in the seeds from working *[1 mark]*.

Page 63 — Asexual Reproduction in Plants

1 a) Runners are rapidly growing stems that grow sideways from the plant above ground *[1 mark]*. The runners take root, producing new plants that begin to grow *[1 mark]*.
  b) Because the strawberry plant's offspring are clones of the parent plant/genetically identical to the parent *[1 mark]*.
2 a) E.g. she wants to ensure that the offspring will have exactly the same characteristics as the parent plants *[1 mark]*, which they wouldn't if she allowed the parent plants to reproduce sexually *[1 mark]*.
  b) E.g. taking cuttings *[1 mark]*

Page 64 — Human Reproductive Systems

1 a) X: Vas deferens/sperm duct *[1 mark]*
   Y: Urethra *[1 mark]*
  b) To produce liquid that is mixed with sperm to make semen *[1 mark]*.
  c) E.g.

[1 mark for an arrow pointing to either of the testes.]
2 a) Any two from: e.g. extra facial/body hair / development of muscles / enlargement of penis/testes / production of sperm / breaking/deepening of voice *[2 marks]*
  b) i) oestrogen *[1 mark]*
   ii) E.g. growth of extra pubic/underarm hair / widening of the hips / development of breasts / start of periods/release of ova *[1 mark]*
3 Any three from: e.g. the ovary *[1 mark]* produces ova (eggs) and sex hormones *[1 mark]*. / The fallopian tube (oviduct) *[1 mark]* carries the ovum (egg) from the ovary to the uterus (womb) *[1 mark]*. / The uterus (womb) *[1 mark]* can contain a growing embryo *[1 mark]*. / The endometrium *[1 mark]* provides a good blood supply for embryo implantation *[1 mark]*. / The vagina *[1 mark]* is where sperm are deposited *[1 mark]*.

Page 65 — The Menstrual Cycle and Pregnancy

1 D *[1 mark]*
2 a) To allow food, oxygen and waste substances to be exchanged between mother and fetus *[1 mark]*.
  b) It protects the fetus against knocks/bumps *[1 mark]*.
3 a) A, because a rise in the level of oestrogen results in the release of an egg *[1 mark]*.

b) The uterus lining is thickest during the second half of the cycle/after the egg is released/between days 14 and 28 *[1 mark]*. This is because the uterus is preparing to receive a fertilised egg/zygote *[1 mark]*.

Pages 66-67 — Genetic Diagrams

1 a) They have brown hair *[1 mark]*.
b) heterozygous *[1 mark]*
2 a)

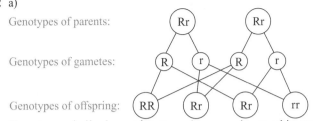

Genotypes of parents:

Genotypes of gametes:

Genotypes of offspring:

Phenotypes of offspring: red eyes red eyes red eyes white eyes

[1 mark for correct genotypes of the parents, 1 mark for correct genotypes of gametes, 1 mark for correct genotypes and phenotypes of offspring]

b) i) 1 in 4 / 25% / 0.25 / ¼ *[1 mark]*
ii) 75% of the offspring are likely to have red eyes
(75 ÷ 100) × 60 = **45** *[2 marks for the correct answer, otherwise 1 mark for 75 ÷ 100, 75%, ¾ or 0.75]*

3 a) AA, Aa *[1 mark]*
b) (7 ÷ 12) × 100 *[1 mark]* = **58%** *[1 mark]*
c) i) E.g.

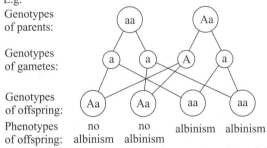

Genotypes of parents:

Genotypes of gametes:

Genotypes of offspring:

Phenotypes of offspring: no albinism no albinism albinism albinism

[1 mark for correct genotypes of both parents, 1 mark for correct genotypes of gametes, 1 mark for correct genotypes and phenotypes of offspring]

ii) 50% *[1 mark]*
iii) Fertilisation is random/the genetic diagram only shows the probability of the outcome, so the numbers of offspring produced will not always be exactly in those proportions *[1 mark]*.

Page 68 — More Genetic Diagrams

1 a)

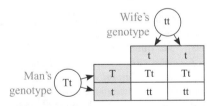

Wife's genotype

Man's genotype

Offspring's phenotypes:
Tt genotype has syndrome. tt genotype does not have syndrome.
[1 mark for correct genotypes of both parents, 1 mark for correct genotypes of gametes (shown in grey boxes), 1 mark for correct genotypes and phenotypes of children]

b) 1 in 2 / 50% / 0.5 / ½ *[1 mark]*

2 a) Codominant *[1 mark]*, because the spotted flowers display both red and white characteristics *[1 mark]*.
b)

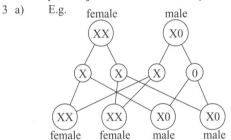

Parent 1

Parent 2

[1 mark for correct genotypes of both parents, 1 mark for correct genotypes of gametes (shown in grey boxes), 1 mark for correct genotypes of offspring]

c) 1 : 2 : 1 (red : spotted : white flowers) *[1 mark]*

Pages 69-70 — Family Pedigrees and Sex Determination

1 Dd *[1 mark]*. Polydactyly is a dominant disorder, so if she was DD all of her children would be affected *[1 mark]*.
2 a) Susan: ff *[1 mark]*, Anne: FF *[1 mark]*, Libby: Ff *[1 mark]*
In the exam, make sure you write your 'fs' clearly — the examiner needs to be able to tell which is the capital letter and which is lower case. If they both look the same, the examiner won't know what your answer is and you could lose out on the marks.
b)

	Probability of cystic fibrosis
Baby X	0 / 0%
Baby Y	1 in 4 / 25% / 0.25 / ¼

[1 mark for each correct answer]

3 a) E.g.

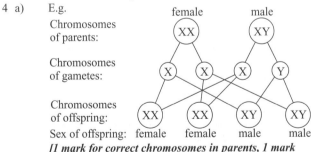

female   male

female female male male

[1 mark for correct chromosomes in gametes, 1 mark for correct chromosomes of offspring, 1 mark for correct sex of offspring]

b) 50% of the offspring are likely to be male
(50 ÷ 100) × 170 = **85** *[2 marks for correct answer, otherwise 1 mark for 50 ÷ 100, 50%, 0.5 or ½]*

4 a) E.g.

female   male

Chromosomes of parents:

Chromosomes of gametes:

Chromosomes of offspring:

Sex of offspring: female female male male
[1 mark for correct chromosomes in parents, 1 mark for correct chromosomes in gametes, 1 mark for correct chromosomes in offspring and the correct sex of offspring]

b) Male children will not inherit the colour blindness allele because they don't inherit an X chromosome from their father *[1 mark]*.
c) 0 / 0% *[1 mark]*
A daughter of this couple would inherit the recessive colour blindness allele from her father, but also a dominant allele from her mother, so she would not be colour-blind.

Page 71 — Variation

1 a) No, because hair colour is controlled by genes *[1 mark]* and identical twins have the same genes *[1 mark]*.

b) The difference in weight must be caused by the environment *[1 mark]*, because the twins have exactly the same genes *[1 mark]*.

In this case, the environment can mean the amount of food each twin eats or the amount of exercise they each do.

c) No, because if they were caused by genes both twins should have the birthmark *[1 mark]*.

2 There is no guarantee that the foal will be a successful racehorse *[1 mark]* because sexual reproduction results in a random combination of genes in the offspring *[1 mark]*, meaning that the foal might not be genetically suited to racing *[1 mark]*. In addition, environmental conditions contribute to how successful the foal is and these cannot be exactly replicated/completely controlled *[1 mark]*.

Page 72 — Evolution and Natural Selection

1 E.g. ancestors of the modern buff tip moth showed variation in their appearance *[1 mark]*. The moths that looked more like broken twigs were less likely to be seen and eaten by predators/more likely to survive *[1 mark]* and so were more likely to reproduce *[1 mark]*. As a result, the alleles that caused the moths to look more like broken twigs were more likely to be passed on to the next generation *[1 mark]*, meaning that over time these genes became increasingly widespread in the population and eventually all buff tip moths resembled a broken twig *[1 mark]*.

2 After the storm, there will be fewer larger seeds available on the island *[1 mark]*. Birds with larger beaks will be less able to get food and seed size will become a selection pressure *[1 mark]*. Small seeds will still be available, so birds with smaller beaks will be better adapted to their environment than the birds with larger beaks *[1 mark]*. This makes birds with smaller beaks more likely to survive and reproduce than birds with larger beaks *[1 mark]*. In turn, this means that the alleles responsible for small beaks are more likely to be passed on to the next generation than the alleles for larger beaks *[1 mark]*. The alleles for smaller beaks will become more common in the population over time and eventually, all the finches in the population will have smaller beaks *[1 mark]*.

Page 73 — Mutations and Antibiotic Resistance

1 a) A rare, random change in an organisms's DNA *[1 mark]* that can be inherited *[1 mark]*.

b) Mutations change the sequence of DNA bases *[1 mark]*, which can change the protein produced by a gene *[1 mark]* and lead to a different phenotype, increasing variation *[1 mark]*.

2 a) natural selection *[1 mark]*

b)

Stage	Order
The gene for methicillin resistance became more common in the population over time.	4
Individual bacteria with the mutated genes were more likely to survive and reproduce in a host being treated with methicillin.	2
Random mutations in the DNA of *Staphylococcus aureus* led to it being less affected by methicillin.	1
The gene for methicillin resistance was passed on to lots of offspring, who also survived and reproduced.	3

[2 marks for all answers in the correct order, otherwise 1 mark for two or more answers in the correct order .]

Section 8 — Ecology and the Environment

Page 74 — Ecosystems and Biodiversity

1 a) Biodiversity is the variety of different species of organisms on Earth, or within an ecosystem *[1 mark]*.

b) A habitat is the place where an organism lives *[1 mark]*.

c) B *[1 mark]*

2 a) E.g. the population of prickly acacia may have increased *[1 mark]* because they grow best when there is plenty of water *[1 mark]*.

b) E.g. the prickly acacia may become distributed over a wider area *[1 mark]* as they may spread into areas that were previously too cold for them *[1 mark]*.

c) E.g. the prickly acacia may compete with the grasses for resources (such as light, water, space and nutrients), causing their populations to decrease *[1 mark]*.

Pages 75-76 — Using Quadrats

1 a) i) To make sure the results are representative of the whole sample area *[1 mark]*.

ii) E.g. divide the field into a grid and place the quadrats at coordinates selected using a random number generator *[1 mark]*.

b) $15 + 13 + 16 + 23 + 26 + 23 + 13 + 12 + 16 + 13 = 170$
$170 \div 10 = $ **17 buttercups per 0.5 m²** *[1 mark]*

c) $17 \times 2 = 34$ per m²
$34 \times 1750 = $ **59 500 buttercups** *[2 marks for the correct answer, otherwise 1 mark for multiplying answer to part d) by 2.]*

d) E.g. by using a larger sample size/data from more quadrats *[1 mark]*.

2 a) E.g. he could have set up a belt transect *[1 mark]* by marking out a line from the wood to the opposite side of the field *[1 mark]*. He then could have placed quadrats at regular intervals/every 2 metres along the line *[1 mark]*, and counted the dandelions in each quadrat *[1 mark]*.

b) The number of dandelions increases with distance from the wood *[1 mark]*.

c) Bill's results are not valid because he hasn't controlled all of the variables *[1 mark]*, so his investigation is not a fair test *[1 mark]*.

d) E.g. different soil moisture levels caused by the stream between the field and the wood *[1 mark]*.

Page 77 — Pyramids of Number, Biomass and Energy

1 a) 4 *[1 mark]*.

b) crab *[1 mark]*

c) decomposers *[1 mark]*

2 a) The concentration of DDT in organisms increases as you go up the trophic levels *[1 mark]*.

b) $13.8 \div 0.04 = $ **345 times**
[2 marks for correct answer, otherwise 1 mark for using 13.8 and 0.04 in calculation]

c) E.g. because DDT is stored in the tissues of animals and a pyramid of biomass represents the mass of the living tissues *[1 mark]*.

Page 78 — Energy Transfer and Food Webs

1 a) $2070 \div 10 = 207$ kJ available to the second trophic level *[1 mark]*
$207 - (90 + 100) = $ **17 kJ** available to Animal A *[1 mark]*

b) Any two from: respiration / heat loss / loss in waste/faeces *[1 mark for each correct answer]*

c) Because energy is lost at each trophic level *[1 mark]*, so there's not enough energy to support more levels *[1 mark]*.

2 The weevils eat platte thistles so could decrease this population, reducing the food available for honeybees *[1 mark]*. If the honeybee population decreases, the amount of wild honey produced will decrease *[1 mark]*.

Page 79 — The Carbon Cycle

1 a) i) photosynthesis *[1 mark]*
   ii) carbon dioxide *[1 mark]*
  b) respiration *[1 mark]*
  c) Microorganisms break down/decompose material from dead organisms *[1 mark]* and return carbon to the air as carbon dioxide through respiration *[1 mark]*.
  d) i) Fossil fuels are formed from dead animals and/or plants which contain carbon *[1 mark]*.
   ii) Carbon is released into the atmosphere as carbon dioxide when fossil fuels are burnt *[1 mark]*.

Page 80 — The Nitrogen Cycle

1 a) C *[1 mark]*
  b) D *[1 mark]*
  c) A *[1 mark]*
2 a) Denitrifying bacteria convert nitrates into nitrogen gas *[1 mark]*, so *P. denitrificans* would reduce the level of nitrates in the lake, which would cause eutrophication to slow down/stop *[1 mark]*. *P. denitrificans* can live in anaerobic conditions, so would be able to work in the oxygen-depleted water *[1 mark]*.
  b) *P. denitrificans* would break down some of the nitrates into nitrogen gas, so less would be available to the rice crop *[1 mark]*, meaning the crop yield would increase by less than if *P. denitrificans* were not present *[1 mark]*.

Page 81 — Air Pollution

1 a) Carbon monoxide combines with haemoglobin in red blood cells and prevents them from carrying oxygen *[1 mark]*.
  b) E.g. through car emissions *[1 mark]*.
2 a) $(9.8 + 9.4 + 7.1) \div 3 = $ **8.8 micrograms/m³**
    [2 marks for correct answer, otherwise 1 mark for adding the individual site results together and dividing by 3]
  b) E.g. by making repeat measurements at each site *[1 mark]*.
  c) Sulfur dioxide mixes with water vapour in the atmosphere/clouds to form sulfuric acid that falls as acid rain *[1 mark]*. Acid rain can kill organisms living in lakes/aquatic ecosystems because it makes the water more acidic *[1 mark]*. Acid rain can kill trees because the acid damages the leaves/releases toxic substances from the soil that make it hard for trees to take up nutrients *[1 mark]*.

Page 82 — The Greenhouse Effect

1 E.g. industrial processes / burning fossil fuels / transportation / deforestation *[1 mark]*
   E.g. growing rice / cattle rearing *[1 mark]*
   E.g. use of fertilisers / industrial processes / transportation *[1 mark]*
2 a) Greenhouse gases absorb energy that is radiated away from the Earth *[1 mark]* and re-radiate it in all directions, including back to Earth *[1 mark]*.
  b) E.g. it would be very cold at night *[1 mark]*.
  c) Increasing levels of greenhouse gases in the atmosphere *[1 mark]* have enhanced the greenhouse effect *[1 mark]*, causing the Earth to warm up, which is global warming *[1 mark]*.
  d) E.g. melting ice caps/glaciers *[1 mark]* could lead to flooding of human towns/settlements *[1 mark]*. / Changing rainfall patterns *[1 mark]* could lead to changing crop growth patterns/less food being grown *[1 mark]*.

Pages 83-84 — Water Pollution and Deforestation

1 a) As the concentration of nitrates increased, the number of fish per cubic metre decreased *[1 mark]*.
  b) E.g. increased use of fertilisers. / Increased runoff/leaching of fertilisers due to higher rainfall *[1 mark]*.
  c) i) Eutrophication *[1 mark]*.
   ii) Increased levels of nitrates provide extra nutrients for algae on the surface of the river, causing them to grow fast *[1 mark]*, blocking out the light and preventing plants below from photosynthesising *[1 mark]*. The plants start to die, providing food for microorganisms *[1 mark]* which increase in number and use up all the oxygen in the water *[1 mark]*. Fish need oxygen, so as less oxygen is available the fish start to die, and their numbers decrease *[1 mark]*.
2 The number of microorganisms increases downstream of the sewage pipe *[1 mark]*. The sewage provides extra nutrients, causing rapid algal growth *[1 mark]*. The algae block out light from plants, causing them to die *[1 mark]*. The dead plants provide food for microorganisms, causing the number of microorganisms to increase *[1 mark]*.
3 a) When forests are cut down, less carbon dioxide is removed from the atmosphere by photosynthesising trees *[1 mark]*. The trees that are cut down are often burnt to clear the land, which releases carbon dioxide into the atmosphere *[1 mark]*. Any trees that aren't burned are decomposed by microorganisms, which release carbon dioxide through respiration *[1 mark]*. All of these processes increase the level of carbon dioxide (a greenhouse gas) in the atmosphere, which contributes to global warming *[1 mark]*.
  b) When trees are cut down, evapotranspiration is reduced *[1 mark]*. This results in a reduction in precipitation/rainfall, which leads to a drier climate *[1 mark]*.
  c) Tree roots help hold the soil together *[1 mark]*. When trees are removed soil can be eroded/washed away by rain *[1 mark]*.
  d) Trees take up nutrients from the soil and return them when fallen leaves decay/the trees die *[1 mark]*. When trees are removed, the nutrients are washed out of/leached from the soil by rain and are not replaced, leaving infertile soil *[1 mark]*.

Section 9 — Use of Biological Resources

Page 85 — Increasing Crop Yields

1 a) To increase her crop yield [*1 mark*] as she can create the ideal conditions for photosynthesis inside a polythene tunnel *[1 mark]* and it's easier to keep her plants free from diseases/pests *[1 mark]*.
  b) i) Fertiliser C *[1 mark]* because strawberry yield was highest with this fertiliser for 4 out of the 5 years/in total over the 5 years/on average over the five years *[1 mark]*.
   ii) Fertilisers contain some of the elements that crops need in order to grow and to carry out life processes *[1 mark]*. These elements may be missing from the soil, so fertilisers are used to replace them *[1 mark]* or to add more to the soil *[1 mark]*.
2 a) E.g. as the size of the pest population decreases the crop yield increases *[1 mark]*, because less of the crop is damaged by the pests *[1 mark]*.
  b) Year 4 *[1 mark]*
You can tell that the pesticide started to be used in year 4 because it was in this year that the average pest population dropped dramatically from the level seen the year before.

Page 86 — Bacteria and Making Yoghurt

1 a) B *[1 mark]*
  b) lactic acid *[1 mark]*
2 a) Aseptic conditions mean that unwanted microbes are removed *[1 mark]*. This increases product yield, as the microorganisms aren't competing with other organisms *[1 mark]*. It also means the product doesn't get contaminated (with other microbes/products from other microbes) *[1 mark]*.
  b) i) To supply oxygen for aerobic respiration *[1 mark]*.
   ii) To prevent the enzymes in the microorganisms from becoming denatured *[1 mark]*.

Answers

144

Page 87 — Yeast and Making Bread

1 a) carbon dioxide *[1 mark]*
   b) E.g. by counting the bubbles of carbon dioxide produced over a certain amount of time *[1 mark]*.
   c) i) E.g. she could stand the test tube containing the yeast suspension in a water bath set at different temperatures *[1 mark]*.
     ii) It would increase the rate of respiration *[1 mark]*.
2 Enzymes break down the carbohydrates in the flour into sugars *[1 mark]*. The yeast then uses these sugars in aerobic respiration and then anaerobic respiration (when the oxygen is used up) *[1 mark]*, which both produce carbon dioxide *[1 mark]*. The carbon dioxide produced is trapped in bubbles in the dough *[1 mark]*. These bubbles of gas expand, causing the dough to rise *[1 mark]*.

Page 88 — Selective Breeding

1 The tall and dwarf wheat plants could be cross-bred *[1 mark]*. The best of the offspring/the offspring with the highest grain yield and highest bad-weather resistance could then be cross-bred *[1 mark]*, and this process repeated over several generations *[1 mark]*.
2 a) E.g. yes, because the average milk yield has increased over the generations *[1 mark]*.
   b) 5750 − 5000 = 750 litres per year per cow *[2 marks for correct answer, otherwise 1 mark for correct calculation.]*

Page 89 — Fish Farming

1 a) i) E.g. wasted food / excrement / parasites *[1 mark]*
     ii) E.g. pH / temperature / oxygen level *[1 mark]*
   b) E.g. to protect the fish from predators / interspecific predation *[1 mark]*.
   c) i) Intraspecific predation is where organisms eat individuals of the same species *[1 mark]*.
     ii) E.g. it can be avoided on a fish farm by keeping small fish separate from big fish / providing regular food *[1 mark]*.
   d) The fish farmers could use selective breeding *[1 mark]*.
2 E.g. rear some fish in cages in the sea and some in tanks. Use the same species and age of fish in both places. Make sure the fish in both places have the same access to and type of food and the same protection from predators. Measure the mass of the fish in each place at the start of the experiment and again after three months. Repeat the experiment at least three times and calculate the mean change in mass in each place.
   [1 mark for stating that some fish will be raised in cages in the sea and some in tanks, 1 mark for stating that all the fish used will be the same age and species, 1 mark for describing one control variable, 1 mark for describing a second control variable, 1 mark for stating how long the fish will be allowed to grow for (e.g. three months), 1 mark for stating what will be measured (e.g. the mass of the fish), 1 mark for stating that repeats should be carried out. Maximum 6 marks available.]

Pages 90-91 — Genetic Engineering

1 The tomato shown will contain genes transferred from another species *[1 mark]*.
2 a) A *[1 mark]*
   b) plasmid *[1 mark]*
   c) DNA that is formed by joining different pieces of DNA together *[1 mark]*.
   d) The recombinant DNA is inserted into bacterial cells *[1 mark]*. These bacteria will use the inserted DNA to produce human insulin *[1 mark]*. The bacteria are grown in huge numbers in a fermenter to produce large amounts of human insulin *[1 mark]*.

3 a) i) So that both types of crop experienced the same conditions *[1 mark]*, meaning it was a fair test *[1 mark]*.
     ii) E.g. the researchers could carry out a large number of repeats *[1 mark]*.
   b) E.g. yes, because for three out of the four kinds of crop grown, more butterflies and bees were found on the normal crops compared to the GM crops *[1 mark]*.
   c) Any two from: e.g. transplanted genes may pass into other organisms in the environment. / GM crops could adversely affect food chains. / GM crops could adversely affect human health. / GM crops might create unforeseen problems, which could get passed on to future generations *[2 marks]*.
   d) E.g. it would mean that farmers could produce bigger crop yields, as less of their crops would be affected by pests *[1 mark]*.

Page 92 — Cloning

1 a) E.g. cloning means that the useful genetic characteristics are always passed on, which doesn't always happen in breeding. / Farmers don't have to wait for the breeding season. / Infertile animals can be cloned *[1 mark]*.
   b) E.g. cloned animals might not be as healthy as normal ones. / Cloning is a new science and might have consequences we're not yet aware of. / At the moment it's difficult/ time-consuming/expensive *[1 mark]*.
2 a) D *[1 mark]*
   b) i) Small pieces of a plant/explants are taken from the tips of the plant's stems and side shoots *[1 mark]*. The small pieces of plant/explants are sterilised and grown in vitro *[1 mark]* on nutrient medium *[1 mark]*. Cells in the small pieces of plant/explants divide and grow into a plant *[1 mark]*.
     ii) E.g. lots of plants with desirable characteristics can be grown *[1 mark]*.

Practice Paper 1B

1 a) i) haploid *[1 mark]*
     ii) B *[1 mark]*
     iii) B *[1 mark]*
   b) At fertilisation a male gamete fuses with a female gamete *[1 mark]* to form a zygote *[1 mark]*. The zygote then undergoes cell division and develops into an embryo *[1 mark]*.
2 a) oxygen *[1 mark]*
Remember, plants give off oxygen when they photosynthesise.
   b) The volume of gas collected would decrease *[1 mark]* because when the lamp is turned off the light intensity will decrease *[1 mark]*, so the rate of photosynthesis will decrease too *[1 mark]*.
   c) Carbon dioxide is needed for photosynthesis *[1 mark]*, so adding it to the water ensures that the rate of photosynthesis is not limited by a lack of carbon dioxide *[1 mark]*.
   d) The enzymes needed for photosynthesis work more slowly at low temperatures, so the rate of photosynthesis will be slower at low temperatures *[1 mark]*. But if the temperature is too high, the enzymes are denatured so photosynthesis won't happen *[1 mark]*. The temperature could be controlled, for example, by putting the beaker into a warm water bath to keep the temperature constant *[1 mark]*.
   e) i) B *[1 mark]*
     ii) Yes. The pondweed has been photosynthesising, so it will have produced glucose, which is stored as starch *[1 mark]*.
3 a) Any three from: they provide a large surface area so that digested food is absorbed into the blood quickly. / They have a single permeable layer of surface cells to assist quick absorption. / They have a very good blood supply to assist quick absorption. / They have a lacteal for absorbing fats *[3 marks]*.

Answers

b) Amino acids are absorbed into the blood by active transport *[1 mark]*. They are absorbed against the concentration gradient using energy (transferred from respiration) *[1 mark]*.
The diagram shows more amino acids in the blood than in the gut, so they must be absorbed by active transport.

c) i) To carry oxygen from the lungs to the cells *[1 mark]*.
   ii) They have a large surface area for absorbing oxygen *[1 mark]*. They don't have a nucleus, so they have more room to carry oxygen *[1 mark]*. They contain lots of haemoglobin, which combines reversibly with oxygen in the lungs to become oxyhaemoglobin *[1 mark]*.

4 a) i)

[1 mark for drawing the plant shoots growing towards the hole in the box]

   ii) Light coming through the hole in the box *[1 mark]* caused more auxin to accumulate on the shaded sides of the shoots *[1 mark]*. This made the cells on the shaded sides of the plants grow/elongate faster *[1 mark]*, so the shoots bent towards the light *[1 mark]*.

b) A *[1 mark]*

5 a) i) E.g.
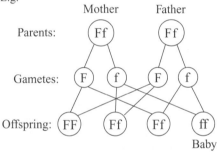

[1 mark for showing that the parents both have the Ff genotype, 1 mark for showing the gametes' genotypes as F or f, 1 mark for correctly showing all three possible genotypes of the couple's offspring.]

The parents must both have one copy of the recessive allele for cystic fibrosis — so they're both Ff.
In a question like this, the marks are allocated for the correct genotypes of the parents, gametes and offspring. It doesn't matter what type of genetic diagram you draw as long as it shows this information — so you could have drawn a Punnett square.

   ii) Homozygous, because he has two alleles the same/both of his alleles are recessive *[1 mark]*.

b) 1 in 4 / 25% *[1 mark]*

c) Ff *[1 mark]*. Ian has the genotype Ff, so Leina must also have the genotype Ff in order for her children to inherit the genotypes: FF (Carys), ff (Beth) and Ff (Alfie) *[1 mark]*.

d) Environmental variation *[1 mark]*. The scar would have been caused by an environmental factor rather than being determined by genes *[1 mark]*.

6 a) The dark variety is better camouflaged in soot-polluted areas, so it is less likely to be eaten by predators *[1 mark]*. This means more dark moths survive to breed *[1 mark]* and pass the gene(s) for this characteristic on to the next generation *[1 mark]*. As this process continues over time, the dark variety of moth becomes more common *[1 mark]*.

It makes sense that if an organism blends in with its background it'll be harder for predators to spot it.

b) Town B is the most polluted because it contains a higher percentage of dark moths *[1 mark]*.

c) 77% − 25% = **52%**
[2 marks for correct answer, otherwise 1 mark for correctly reading 77% and 25% off the graph]

7 a) Mean change in mass = (−0.78 + −0.81 + −0.82) ÷ 3
= **−0.80 g**
[2 marks for correct answer, otherwise 1 mark for adding together 3 values and dividing by 3]

b)
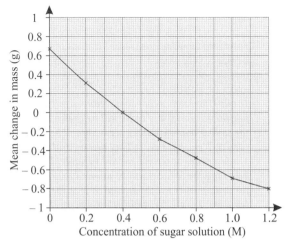

[1 mark for choosing a suitable scale, 1 mark for using straight lines to join the points, 1 mark for having axes labelled correctly (with correct units), 1 mark for having the axes the correct way round, 2 marks for all points plotted correctly (or 1 mark for at least 5 points plotted correctly). Plotting marks may still be given if an incorrect answer to 7 a) has been plotted correctly.]

c) The concentration of sugar inside the original potatoes was approximately 0.4 M *[1 mark]*. This is the point where there was no change in weight of the potato cylinders, therefore no net movement of water, because the concentrations on both sides of the (partially permeable) membrane were the same *[1 mark]*.

d) To give more reliable results *[1 mark]*.
Repeating an experiment also means that you should be able to spot any glaring errors — like reading the balance wrongly in this experiment.

8 a) i) D *[1 mark]*
   ii) 130 J *[1 mark]*
Tertiary consumers are the third consumers in a food chain — so in this case the tertiary consumers are the snakes.

   iii) E.g. the population of plants may increase *[1 mark]* because there are fewer grasshoppers to feed on them *[1 mark]*. / The population of mice may decrease *[1 mark]* because there is less food available for them *[1 mark]*.

b) D, because the biomass of the organisms decreases at each trophic level *[1 mark]* and the bars on this pyramid get smaller at each trophic level *[1 mark]*.

c) (130 ÷ 1100) × 100% = **11.8%**
[2 marks for correct answer, otherwise 1 mark for using 130 ÷ 1100 in working]

d) Energy is lost at each level of a food chain *[1 mark]*. After about five levels the amount of energy being passed on is not sufficient to support another level of organisms *[1 mark]*.

9 a) Gas A = oxygen *[1 mark]*, Gas B = carbon dioxide *[1 mark]*

b) Any three from: they provide a large surface area for diffusion to occur across. / They have a moist lining for gases to dissolve in. / They have thin walls, so gases only have to diffuse a short distance. / They have permeable walls so gases can diffuse across easily. / They have a good blood supply to maintain a high concentration gradient *[3 marks]*.

c) The intercostal muscles and diaphragm relax *[1 mark]*. This causes the volume of the thorax to decrease *[1 mark]*, which increases the pressure in the lungs *[1 mark]*, so air is forced out *[1 mark]*.

10   E.g. plant some lettuce seeds outside and some under a polythene tunnel. Ensure that the lettuce seeds are of the same variety and plant them in compost taken from the same batch. Allow the lettuces to grow for 28 days, making sure that the lettuces in both environments receive the same amount of water and fertiliser during this time. After 28 days take three lettuces from outside and three lettuces from the polythene tunnel and measure the mass of each lettuce using a balance. Calculate the average mass of the lettuces grown outside and compare it to the average mass of those grown under the polythene tunnel.

[1 mark for stating that some lettuces will be grown in a polythene tunnel and some will be grown outside, 1 mark for stating that the lettuce seeds should be of the same variety, 1 mark for describing one control variable, 1 mark for describing a second control variable, 1 mark for stating how long the lettuces will be allowed to grow for, 1 mark for stating what will be measured (e.g. the mass of the lettuces), 1 mark for stating that repeats should be carried out (e.g. by measuring the mass of three lettuces from each environment). Maximum 6 marks available.]

You're not expected to know exactly how to do this investigation or to have done it before. This type of question is designed to test your knowledge of experimental skills, even when the scenario is unfamiliar to you.

11 a)   Beaker B was low in nitrates *[1 mark]*. Nitrates are needed for making amino acids/proteins *[1 mark]*, which are essential for growth *[1 mark]*.

    b)   It would have yellow leaves *[1 mark]* because without magnesium, plants can't make the chlorophyll that gives them their green colour *[1 mark]*.

    c)   Any two from: e.g. the amount of light shining on each beaker / the level of other substances in the mineral solution / the size of the beakers / the amount of air available / the amount of water available / the temperature of the beakers *[2 marks]*.

12 a) i)   E.g. the graph suggests that the more cigarettes male doctors smoke per day, the more likely they are to die from coronary heart disease *[1 mark]*. The male doctors who give up smoking are less likely to die from coronary heart disease than those who do smoke *[1 mark]*. The male doctors who have never smoked are the least likely to die from coronary heart disease *[1 mark]*.

      ii)   E.g. you could include women as well as men in the study. / You could use a sample of people from several different professions *[1 mark]*.

    b)   Any two from: e.g. smoking damages the walls inside the alveoli *[1 mark]*, reducing the surface area for gas exchange/ leading to diseases like emphysema *[1 mark]*. / The tar in cigarettes damages the cilia in the lungs/trachea *[1 mark]*, leading to the build-up of mucus/increasing the risk of chest infections *[1 mark]*. / Tar irritates the bronchi and bronchioles, *[1 mark]* leading to excess mucus/a smoker's cough/chronic bronchitis *[1 mark]*. / Tobacco smoke contains carcinogens *[1 mark]*, which can lead to lung cancer *[1 mark]*.

13 a)   amount/rate of exercise *[1 mark]*

    b)   129 beats/min (accept 128-130 beats/min) *[1 mark]*

    c)   8 – 2 = **6 minutes** *[1 mark]*

    d)   The student's heart rate increases during exercise *[1 mark]*. This is because when he exercises he needs more energy, so he respires more *[1 mark]*. Respiration increases the amount of carbon dioxide in his blood *[1 mark]*, which is detected by receptors (in his aorta and carotid artery) *[1 mark]*. The receptors send signals to his brain, which signals for his heart rate to increase *[1 mark]*.

e) i)   glucose + oxygen → carbon dioxide + water (+ energy)
[1 mark for glucose + oxygen on the left-hand side of the equation, 1 mark for carbon dioxide + water (+ energy) on the right.]

    ii)   E.g. aerobic respiration releases more energy than anaerobic respiration. / Aerobic respiration doesn't cause lactic acid to build up in the muscles, but anaerobic respiration does. / Aerobic respiration produces lots/32 molecules of ATP per molecule of glucose, whereas anaerobic respiration produces much fewer/2 molecules of ATP *[1 mark]*.

Practice Paper 2B

1 a)   E.g. in developed countries people generally have a diet containing enough of the vitamins they need. / Sources of dietary vitamin A are affordable to a majority of people in developed countries. / Farming is more reliable, so the availability of foods containing vitamin A is likely to be more constant. / Healthcare is more widely available, so a lack of dietary vitamin A is more likely to be treated. *[1 mark]*

    b) i)   E.g. liver *[1 mark]*

      ii)   C *[1 mark]*

    c)   E.g. it contains genes transferred from other species — a maize plant and a soil bacterium *[1 mark]*.

    d)   E.g. because it is a substance/compound which is converted into vitamin A inside the body. / Because it is substance/ compound which is needed early on in the chemical pathway that produces vitamin A. / Because it is a precursor to vitamin A. *[1 mark]*

    e)   Any two from: e.g. bacteria can be genetically modified to produce insulin. / Crops can be genetically modified to be resistant to insect pests/herbicides. / Animals can be genetically modified to produce human proteins/antibodies (in their milk). *[2 marks]*

    f)   150 ÷ 70 = 2.14...
2.14... × 100 = **214 g** *[2 marks for the correct answer, otherwise 1 mark for using 2.14... in calculation]*

    g)   E.g. by growing Golden Rice, farmers grow their own source of vitamin A and they can earn money by selling any surplus rice *[1 mark]*, whereas regularly buying tablets is likely to be more expensive and no income can be made *[1 mark]*.

    h)   E.g. they don't have to buy new seed at the start of a growing season *[1 mark]* so it reduces their costs *[1 mark]*.

2 a)   B — nitrifying bacteria *[1 mark]*
C — nitrogen-fixing bacteria *[1 mark]*
D — denitrifying bacteria *[1 mark]*

    b)   They decompose/break down dead plant and animal matter/ waste, releasing carbon dioxide back into the atmosphere *[1 mark]* as they respire *[1 mark]*.

3 a)   At point 9/Between points 8 and 9 *[1 mark]* because the oxygen level is lowest at point 9 *[1 mark]*.

    b)   The population size at point 1 would be larger than at point 10 *[1 mark]*.

    c)   The sewage provides extra nutrients, causing rapid algal growth *[1 mark]*. The algae block out the light, causing plants below to die *[1 mark]*. The dead plants provide food for microorganisms, causing the number of microorganisms to increase *[1 mark]*. The microorganisms then deplete/use up the oxygen in the water *[1 mark]*.

    d)   E.g. oxygen-depletion near the source of the pollution has caused the death of fish and other animals in the water *[1 mark]*. This means there's little/nothing for the herons to feed on in this area *[1 mark]*.

    e)   9 – 3.5 = **5.5 mg/l** *[1 mark]*

Answers

4 a)   E.g.

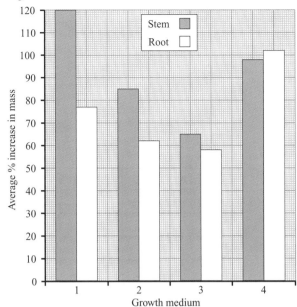

[1 mark for a bar chart covering at least half of the grid, 1 mark for correctly labelling the axes, including units, 1 mark for correctly labelling stem and root columns or including a key, 1 mark for plotting the points by using bars drawn with straight lines, 1 mark for correctly plotted points]

b)   The combination of stem tissue and growth medium number 1 gave the best results *[1 mark]*, as this combination had the highest average percentage increase in tissue mass *[1 mark]*.

c)   Any two from: e.g. the temperature in the incubator *[1 mark]* / the size of the tissue samples/blocks *[1 mark]* / the volume of growth medium used *[1 mark]*.

d)   D *[1 mark]*

e)   Any three from: sexual reproduction involves the fusion of male and female gametes, asexual reproduction doesn't *[1 mark]*. / Sexual reproduction involves two parents, asexual reproduction involves one parent *[1 mark]*. / There is mixing of genetic information in sexual reproduction, but not in asexual reproduction *[1 mark]*. / Asexual reproduction produces clones of the parents, sexual reproduction doesn't *[1 mark]*.

5 a)   pituitary gland *[1 mark]*

b)   FSH causes an egg to mature in one of the ovaries *[1 mark]*. It also stimulates the ovaries to produce oestrogen *[1 mark]*. Oestrogen causes the lining of the uterus to grow, and stimulates the release of LH / inhibits the release of FSH *[1 mark]*. LH stimulates the release of an egg/ovulation *[1 mark]*. Progesterone maintains the lining of the uterus during the second half of the menstrual cycle *[1 mark]*. The production of progesterone inhibits the release of LH and FSH *[1 mark]*.

6 a)   Because the A and T bases in a DNA molecule always pair up with each other (complementary base-pairing) *[1 mark]*.

b)   nucleus *[1 mark]*

c)   four *[1 mark]*

d) i)   C *[1 mark]*

ii)   Any two from: e.g. the mutation may have occurred in an unimportant region of DNA. / The mutated codon may still code for the same amino acid so the structure and function of the protein is not affected. / The mutation may have occurred in a recessive allele. *[2 marks]*

7 a)   The starch is broken down into sugars/maltose *[1 mark]*.

b)   To make the experiment a fair test *[1 mark]*.

c)   The time taken for the reaction to complete increases dramatically (from around 7 minutes to 29 minutes) *[1 mark]*. This is because the increasing pH causes the enzyme to change shape/denature *[1 mark]*. This means that the active site no longer matches the shape of the starch, so cannot catalyse its breakdown, and the reaction slows down *[1 mark]*.

d) i)   The result for pH 7 is anomalous *[1 mark]* because the time taken until starch is no longer present is much slower than expected *[1 mark]*.

ii)   E.g. the student may not have used the correct volume of starch solution. / The student may have used a buffer solution with the wrong pH. / The student may have carried out the experiment at a different temperature. / The student may have started timing the experiment too early *[1 mark]*.

8 a)

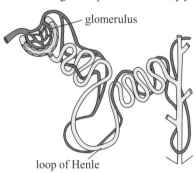

[1 mark for each correct label]

b)   The blood is filtered in the Bowman's capsule and proteins are too big to pass through the membranes *[1 mark]*.

c) i)   Urea is not reabsorbed into the blood, so its concentration increases through the nephron as water is reabsorbed *[1 mark]*.

ii)   The concentration of sugar at point B would be high and there would be no sugar at point C *[1 mark]*, as all sugar is reabsorbed back into the blood in the proximal convoluted tubule/first part of the nephron *[1 mark]*.

d)   ADH increases the permeability of the collecting duct of the nephron *[1 mark]*, causing more water to be reabsorbed into the blood *[1 mark]*.

Answers

Marking Your Papers

- Do both exam papers.

- Use the answers and mark scheme to mark each exam paper.

- Use the tables below to record your marks.

Paper 1

Q	Mark	Q	Mark
1		8	
2		9	
3		10	
4		11	
5		12	
6		13	
7			
	Total		/110

Paper 2

Q	Mark	Q	Mark
1		5	
2		6	
3		7	
4		8	
	Total		/70

- Add together your marks for the two papers to give a total mark out of 180.

> Total Mark = Paper 1 Total + Paper 2 Total
>
> Total Mark = ☐ /180

- If you want to get a **rough idea** of the grade you're working at, we suggest you compare the **total mark** you got to the latest set of grade boundaries.

- Grade boundaries are set for each individual exam, so they're likely to **change** from year to year. You can find the latest set of grade boundaries by going to **www.cgpbooks.co.uk/gcsegradeboundaries**

- Jot down the marks required for each grade in the table below so you don't have to refer back to the website. Use these marks to **estimate your grade**. If you're borderline, don't push yourself up a grade — the real examiners won't.

Total mark required for each grade										
Grade	9	8	7	6	5	4	3	2	1	U
Total mark out of 180										

- Remember, this will only be a **rough guide**, and grade boundaries will be different for different exams, but it should help you to see how you're getting on.